Studies in Comparative Politics

WEST GERMAN POLITICS

STUDIES IN COMPARATIVE POLITICS
published in association with
GOVERNMENT AND OPPOSITION

West German Politics

GEOFFREY K. ROBERTS

Lecturer in Politics
Department of Social Sciences and Economics
University of Technology, Loughborough

TAPLINGER PUBLISHING COMPANY
NEW YORK

First published in the United States in 1972 by
TAPLINGER PUBLISHING CO., INC.
New York, New York

Printed in Great Britain

Library of Congress Catalog Card Number: 77–185875

ISBN 0–8008–8152–4 (paperback edition)
ISBN 0–8008–8151–6 (hardcover edition)

Contents

List of Tables and Diagrams

Preface

West Germany's political system has always been fascinating, but the five years since the formation of the Grand Coalition particularly so. The Grand Coalition itself has now been replaced by the first Government in the history of the Federal Republic to be led by the SPD. The external relations of the Federal Republic have developed in new directions, especially concerning Russia, East Germany and Poland. Internally, the economy, the students and right-wing radicals have all imposed stress on the political system. Meanwhile the environment of West German politics has been changing. In France, de Gaulle has departed, though Franco-German rivalry within the European Economic Community remains. Possibilities of a Russian–American *détente* affect the attitudes of the Federal Republic towards both states. In East Germany, Ulbricht has resigned, though this may not be much of an advantage to West Germany. Within the Federal Republic, the three major parties are all in a state of flux, developing new policies, dealing with problems of internal organisation, and already casting an eye on the election of 1973.

This book is intended as a concise guide to the West German political system, taking account of these recent developments. Two general themes run throughout the book. One is the close interrelationship of German historical development, the political culture and ideas which have been the product of such development, the contemporary political system of the Federal Republic and the issues with which the system has to cope – the 'stuff of politics'. The other theme is the need to explain West German politics as the product of three types of influences: those which are specifically German, those which are European and those which result from West Germany's status as an industrialised society.

Emphasis and selection have not been the easiest of tasks,

but to compensate for necessary compression, especially in some parts of the chapters dealing with history, political institutions and ideologies, a list of more detailed works for further reading is given in the Bibliography. Unfortunately, there is little as yet published in English on political developments since September 1969, which explains my reliance on German sources for the information I have used on recent political changes and current political events. Translations, unless otherwise stated, are my own.

My indebtedness to friends in West Germany for information, hospitality, assistance and helpful criticism is immense, and I am happy to have this opportunity to express my gratitude, especially to the officials of the Federal Government and the political parties, who therefore cannot be named, but who gave information and answered my questions with patience and understanding. More particularly, I must thank Professor Erwin K. Scheuch and his staff at the Institute for Comparative Social Research, University of Köln, where I spent my sabbatical leave in the summer of 1970; the Nuffield Foundation, for a Social Science Fellowship, and the University of Loughborough, for granting study leave, which enabled me to spend my sabbatical leave in Germany; to Dr Max Kaase, for permission to quote from the two papers cited in Chapter 9; to Frau Lanzrath and her staff at *Inter-Nationes*, for the readiness with which they supplied my sometimes unorthodox requests for printed materials on German politics; to the Herren Ulrich and Heine von Alemann (of the University of Bonn and the University of Köln) for their helpful comments and their suggestions concerning certain recent changes in the German political scene; and to Frank Carter, of the University of Loughborough, for co-operation on questions of history and language, and for his collaboration during our research visit in 1969. Finally, my thanks are also due to my wife, Mechthild, for various forms of editorial assistance, and to Inge Pollidori, who did much of the typing.

G.K.R.

Loughborough
May 1971

Introduction

WHY WEST GERMANY?

Germany is important. But Germany is divided.

Despite this division – in part also because of it – to study the politics of the state that has called itself the German Federal Republic is still to study the politics of a major world power, a state that in so many different ways is 'the key to Europe'.

The past and the present have combined to create this importance. Of all the countries that have shaped the world of the 1970s, whether for better or worse, Germany has been the most influential. Its industrial growth, its technological progress, its aggressive foreign relations which led to two world wars, the startlingly rapid economic reconstruction and political rehabilitation of the Federal Republic following the division of Germany into two opposed camps – these alone would mark it for study as being of compelling interest. But, more than this, the German Federal Republic today is a state which occupies a critical position in East–West relationships, in world trade it is second only to the United States, and, above all, its political system is the only successful example of a stable democracy deliberately cultivated in place of a totalitarian dictatorship.

WHY WEST GERMANY'S POLITICS?

In the complex social systems which characterise modern states, it is difficult to make a convincing case for the primacy either of the economic or the political arrangements of society; they interact and relate at so many levels and in so many various modes. Both economics and politics are of such great importance in influencing social change and development that neither can be neglected if any sort of thorough understanding of that society is going to result. But the political aspects of a society, in contrast to the economic aspects, are in many ways more 'controllable', both in the short term and over longer periods of time. There are, and especially in the historical experiences of German society, obvious and outstanding examples of exceptions to this judgement, but in the main it would seem to hold true, whether one thinks of the Kaiser's relationship to Krupp, Hitler's solutions to unemployment, the Adenauer Government and the 'economic miracle', or Brandt's policies towards the Communist bloc and their likely effects on East–West trade.

At the very least, then, it can be claimed that for an understanding of West Germany, in terms of its contemporary situation and its likely development, it is necessary to understand its political system, the way it operates and what its major concerns are. Of course, its geographical and strategic position, cultural background, political history, economy, social patterns and legal system are other major influences, and of course all these affect and in turn are affected by the politics of West Germany, but, if not all the *power*, at least most of the *steering* of West German society is the business of the West German political system.

There is a reverse side to this claim that to understand West Germany, one must understand its politics: to understand contemporary politics, it is becoming more and more essential to know something about the West German political system. This is partly due to the eventful nature of Germany's recent political history, which has left unaffected the politics of few other major nations. It is also due to the very complex, but extremely interesting, structures, policy problems, political groups and personalities which comprise the political system of West Germany today.

THE PATTERN OF THE BOOK

Even a cursory glance at the bookshelves in any library will show that the ways of studying the politics of a country are numerous. The historical background can be emphasised, explaining today's politics as the product of yesterday's experiences, triumphs and errors. The focus can be on a leading personality: for example, much can be learned of Germany's politics between the world wars from Bullock's classical biography of Hitler. The constitution and other relevant legal documents can be used as a skeleton to give a firm structure to an account of the institutions and processes of politics. Or the starting-point can be the social and economic order, with the political as an important and interacting influence.

But whatever method is chosen, in considering just why a particular policy has been introduced, or why a certain political problem exists in a state, and what solutions might be feasible, the ability to produce satisfactory explanations must take some account of four different aspects of politics, four sets of factors that interact to shape the political life of a country. And these four dimensions constitute the major sections of this book.

First, the *historical background* must be considered. No society ever manages to 'invent' its social or political arrangements completely afresh, but rather has to build on the foundations – and the ruins – of its own past. In the case of the German Federal Republic this is even more true than for its neighbours, more true than for France, or the Soviet Union, or the German Democratic Republic (East Germany). Whether discussing the rise and decline of the National Democratic Party (NPD), the influence of refugees on the programmes of the major political parties, the new *Ostpolitik* (Eastern European foreign policy) of the Brandt Government, or the political particularism of Bavaria, much of the relevant information for an appreciation of these problems must be derived from the history of Germany over the past fifty, even the past hundred, years. Other countries participated and suffered through two world wars and the economic depression of the thirties; other countries have faced political instability simultaneously with rapid industrial change; the 'cold war' has been an ever-present factor in the post-war politics of the Soviet Union, Britain, France, the United States and many other countries as well as West Germany. But in no other country are so many of the political decisions, political problems and political institutions, and so much of the political behaviour, directly affected by the experiences of what has gone before.

Second, the current *political institutions* and the functions and processes they perform are very much part of the 'explanation of politics'. In an over-reaction against the sterility of some of the traditional schools of political description, which concentrated excessively on forms, written rules, historical precedent and formal powers, the modern behaviour-oriented political scientists have occasionally fallen into the trap of neglecting the significance of the institutional and formal in their concern with the hidden influences and informal groups in politics. Yet the differences between, say, the legislative procedures of the *Bundestag* and the House of Commons, or between the constitutional powers of the *Bundesrat* and those of the United States Senate, are of political significance in themselves.

But an understanding of this political significance requires the existence of some framework or model which relates the several institutions and their functions to each other, and which emphasises the interactions of the political sector of society with its varied social and physical environment. Some of the most economical and elegant frameworks for such purposes are based on the concept of *system*, and the book's second section draws on such a systems framework, adapted from the analytical works of David Easton and Gabriel Almond, to facilitate consideration of West Germany's political institutions and their functions. In this way, it is intended that the formal and informal functions of, say, the *Bundestag*, the Cabinet and the Chancellor will be related to each other, and the normative prescriptions of the Basic Law can be placed alongside a more behavioural description of how the system actually works, without neglecting either aspect.

How the system actually operates depends to a large extent on the *political culture* of a society: the ideas and ideologies that motivate the actions and demands of politicians and citizens in a polity, and the types and styles of political leadership that have developed. In West Germany, such aspects of political life have become of the greatest political significance, since diagnoses of the failure of Weimar or the success of Hitler in achieving power pointed to (among other things) flaws and weaknesses in the political culture of Germany between the wars. In the twenty-two years since the first *Bundestag* elections, a quite different and novel political culture seems to have become established in West Germany. Democratic ideals are emphasised. Participation is praised as a public virtue. Political education (of the 'right type', of course) is a quite deliberate part of the upbringing of new generations. And there is a great sensitivity to charges of class domination, military interference in politics or attempts by the leaders of industry to convert their economic resources into political power. The third section of this book therefore examines the relationship between the citizen and politics in West Germany, his political socialisation and his political participation. It looks at the political culture of West Germany in the seventies and the ways in which this is affected still by 'the shadow of the past'; it presents the major sets of political ideas from which the values of political groups tend to derive; it investigates the types of political elites and styles of political leadership in the 'new Germany' and their role in influencing or controlling political outcomes.

History, political system, political culture – one might become something of an expert in all these fields, yet still be unable to claim that thorough understanding of German political life that is the prerequisite of what has earlier been called the ability to make satisfactory explanations. The fourth, the dynamic and changing dimension, is the set of *problems and policies* that comprises the 'stuff of politics', the things that the politics of West Germany is all about. In detail, these change from day to day, from parliamentary session to parliamentary session. Any survey of the contents of *Die Zeit* or *Der Spiegel* will demonstrate this. But, at a more general level, it is possible to categorise sets of policies, general areas of continuing political concern, persistent problems of society and the economy that permit a broad analysis to be essayed.

The fourth section of the book, then, is a guide to these areas of political concern, both in order to offer some elucidation of what the politics of West Germany is about, as well as how the system works, and to emphasise what is too easily overlooked: that the institutions and the functions of the system, the political values, political culture and political behaviour of the people, and the political history of tomorrow are all very much shaped by the political concerns of today. It is a two-way process.

PUTTING THE PIECES TOGETHER AGAIN

This is a book about West German politics. But, convenient though it might be for purposes of analytical clarity to concentrate on the study of the political aspects of a society, it is always necessary to 'put Humpty Dumpty together again', to reintegrate knowledge of the political with knowledge of the other relevant aspects of social life in order to gain a more complete understanding of that society. Reminders of this interrelationship of the political and these other aspects will occur throughout the book, and especially in the section on current policies.

Many of these interrelationships will appear to support the beliefs of those who emphasise the particularity of the politics of a country, who claim that the political system of West Germany is the way it is because West German society is what it is, reflecting German history, German culture, even German national character. (But why then, it might be countered, are East and West Germany so very different politically after only twenty-five years of separation?) It is true that, especially to the trained eye of the political scientist, many of the political arrangements and some of the political issues of the Federal Republic are very different from those of France, Italy, the United States or Great Britain. But the search for distinctions must not blind us to the very real similarities between such issues and arrangements and those to be found in other societies, especially in the advanced industrial societies of Europe. The history was certainly distinctive. The forms of the institutions created after the war were affected (in some cases quite deliberately) by British, French and American examples. The political behaviour in a 'European' and 'Western' culture is often very similar in the Federal Republic to political behaviour elsewhere in Western Europe. It is thus not very surprising that many of the major political issues – inflation, industrial relations, social security, environmental pollution, student unrest – should be similar to the political preoccupations of Governments from Dublin to Vienna, from Stockholm to Rome.

It is the identification of such distinctions and the discovery of similarities that make the study of contemporary politics in West Germany interesting. But it is the significance of the politics of West Germany for Germany, Europe and the world that makes its study so fascinating.

MEINEN SCHWIEGERELTERN
GEWIDMET

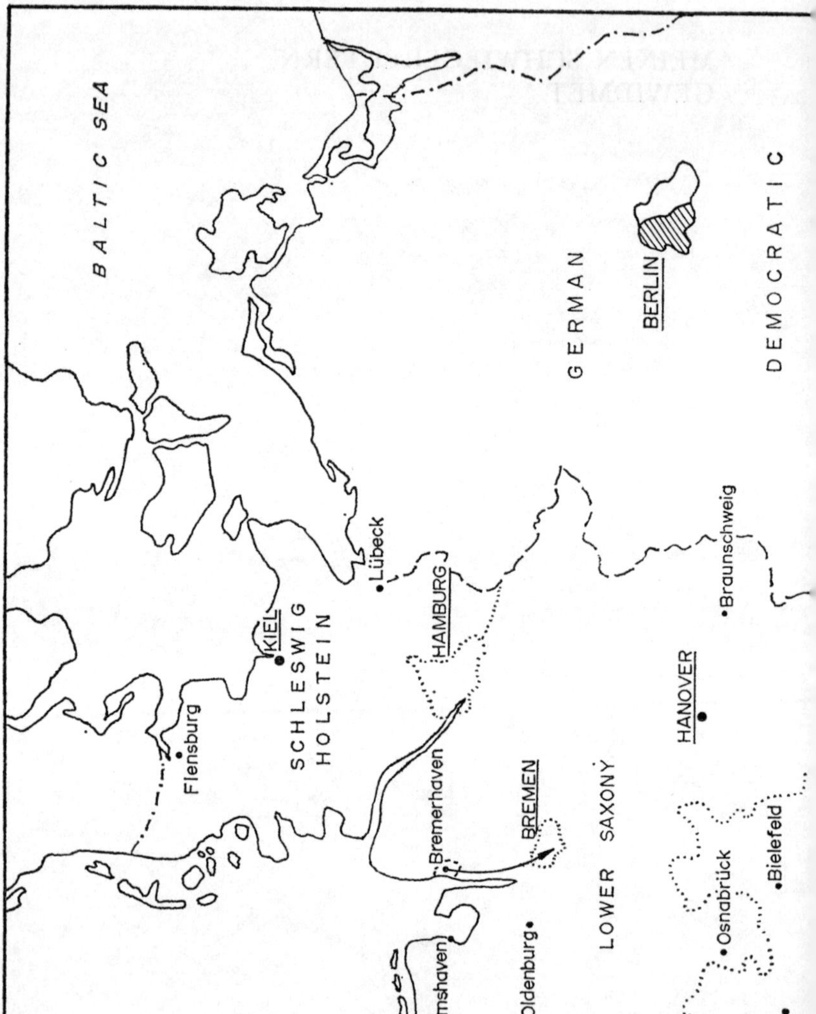
BALTIC SEA
NORTH SEA
GERMAN
DEMOCRATIC
BERLIN
Lübeck
KIEL
SCHLESWIG
HOLSTEIN
Flensburg
HAMBURG
Braunschweig
HANOVER
Bremerhaven
BREMEN
LOWER SAXONY
Oldenburg
Wilhelmshaven
Osnabrück
Bielefeld
Münster

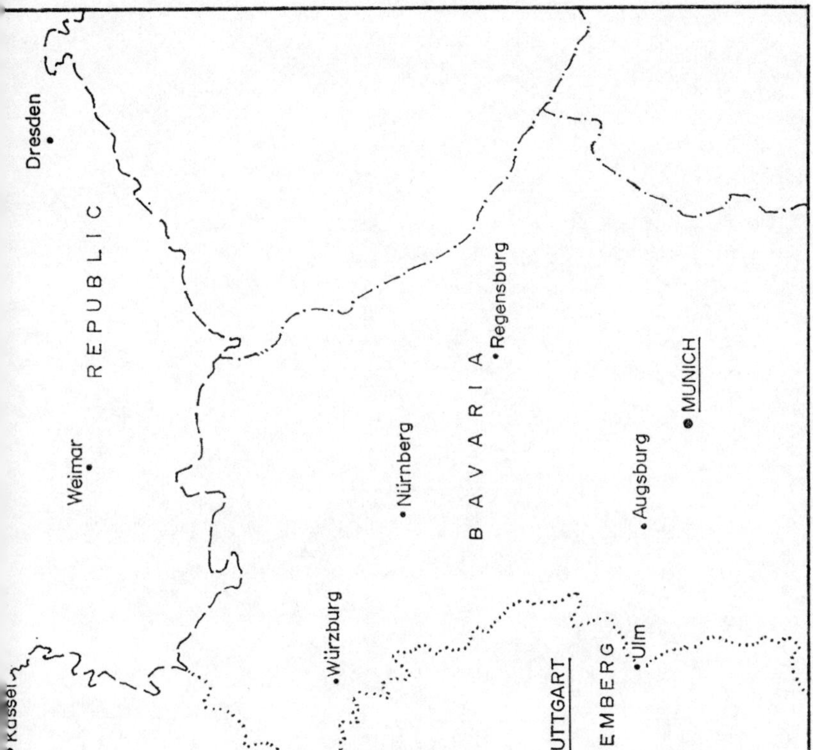

Dresden
REPUBLIC
Weimar
Kassel
Wuppertal
DÜSSELDORF
WESTPHALIA
Cologne
BONN
Rhine
Koblenz
Aachen
HESSE
Frankfurt
WIESBADEN
MAINZ
RHINELAND PFALZ
Trier
SAARLAND
SAARBRÜCKEN
Ludwigshafen
Mannheim
Heidelberg
Darmstadt
Würzburg
Nürnberg
BAVARIA
Regensburg
Augsburg
MUNICH
STUTTGART
BADEN-WÜRTTEMBERG
Ulm
Karlsruhe
Freiburg im Breisgau
R. Rhine

PART ONE
Political History

1 The Empire and the Weimar Republic

GERMANY'S PAST AND THE PRESENT

The history of imperial and Weimar Germany is of great importance to an appreciation of the colossal aberration of the Third *Reich*, and the problems and possibilities of political life in the Federal Republic today. But such a history is made up of a century of complicated developments, significant personalities, rapid social change and cataclysmic international events. Selection is necessary, and attention is focused here on those aspects which relate most particularly to the explanation of political development in Germany, and the contemporary politics of the Federal Republic. Of special importance are the themes of unification and the establishment of the identity of the German state; the course of development of formal political institutions, political groups and the political culture; the major problems with which a succession of Governments have had to cope, and the way in which many of these problems have persisted, in various forms, in modern German politics; and the changes of regime that have occurred: Empire, Republic, Third *Reich*, occupation state and the emergence of Germany's first – seemingly – stable democracy.

UNIFICATION

The 'idea of Germany' did not suddenly emerge for the first time in 1848. It had been a subject for philosophic speculation for many years before then, with the hope that both political liberty and unification could be achieved simultaneously. The surge of liberal nationalism, spreading like an epidemic, which swept Europe in 1848 provided an opportunity for such a liberal-style unification that was eagerly seized in Germany, but disastrously mishandled.

Petitions were presented in 1848 in many of the states, large and small, that were later to comprise the Second Empire.

These petitions called for civil liberties, constitutional democracy, the abolition of vestigial feudal obligations and a parliament for Germany. Frightened princes at first gave in to these demands and promised constitutions; even the most liberal states were not immune. But the key state was Prussia. In March 1848 Frederick William, King of Prussia, made important concessions to the Prussian National Assembly in Berlin. As the year drew on, however, he was encouraged by the Army and the aristocracy to challenge the quarrelling, quibbling Assembly. In November he expelled it from Berlin, and reasserted his autocratic authority, despite the new constitution, which was in any case amended in 1849 to serve as the instrument of autocracy rather than as the weapon of democracy in Prussia.

Frankfurt, not Berlin, was the focus for hopes of German unification in 1848, for here a German National Assembly met in May to draw up a constitution for a federal Germany. In spite of – or perhaps because of – its idealism, the predominance of intellectuals among its membership, and its nationalist fervour, it could overcome neither the reluctance of the princes to relinquish their sovereignty to an emperor, nor the demoralising effects of the defeats of liberal movements throughout Europe. When, ultimately, the Assembly agreed to offer the crown of Germany to Frederick William in March 1849, he was again the autocrat of Prussia, and able to refuse with contempt a crown that came from the people, whose legitimacy he would not recognise.

But, thanks to Bismarck, a Prussian king did accept the imperial crown twenty years later, though from the princes rather than from the people. Otto von Bismarck had acquired an early reputation as a monarchist and a reactionary in the crisis days of March 1848, when a civil war had seemed the only alternative to the King's acceptance of liberal demands. Bismarck had advised resistance, but on that occasion his advice had gone unheeded. He came to prominence in 1862, when a liberal majority in the Prussian Diet (lower house) attempted to exert parliamentary control over military appropriations. King William could see no alternative to submission to this claim of parliamentary control, even though the claim struck at the very foundation of Prussian autocracy. The King was saved from humiliation by his appointment of Bismarck as Chancellor. Bismarck stood firm against the Diet, despite the requirements of the constitution; he raised taxes and spent money without parliamentary sanction (though this was obtained retrospectively) and proceeded to use his dominant position to create a unified Germany under Prussian hegemony. After interfering with advantage in the Schleswig-Holstein question, he decided to eliminate Austria's rival claims to dominate a unified Germany by waging a war against her in 1866. With Austria defeated, Bismarck arranged for his now-enlarged Prussia to join with other states in a North German Federation (1867). From this, it was but a short step to uniting the remaining southern states such as Württemberg and Bavaria in a single federal union. Bismarck arranged his foreign policies so that, four years after the defeat of Austria, he could seize the opportunity offered by France's bellicosity to force France into war, with the southern German states allied to Prussia and her northern neighbours. The victory of this Prussian alliance over France led to the accession of those southern states to the federation, which thus became the Second *Reich* (Empire). Germany was unified, but was neither liberal nor democratic. It was an expression of Prussian expansion rather than a voluntary union of equal partners.

IMPERIAL GERMANY

What sort of state was this new Germany? It was, first of all, an autocratic state when, in other industrialising countries, democracy was making rapid progress. This autocracy stemmed from the dominance of Prussia, resulting from her initiatives in forming the new Empire, her size and economic and military power relative to the other states (and reflected in Prussia's allocation of about one-third of the seats in the Federal Council), but above all it was protected by the coincidence of position accorded under the constitution to the King of Prussia as Kaiser, which meant also the appointment of the Minister-President of Prussia as Imperial Chancellor. Add to this the personality of Bismarck as the first Chancellor, and it is clear that the new Germany was ruled in reality as a Prussian empire.

The Second *Reich* was also a federation, with a very real division of powers between the *Reich* and the constituent states. In some of those states the gains of the liberals were preserved in the constitutions and political practices of the period, to provide experience and example for later constitution-builders. But until his forced resignation in 1890, Bismarck was the architect of German, as well as Prussian, policy in the important spheres of defence, foreign policy, relations between the Government and the political parties, and the social legislation designed to cope with the pressures caused by industrialisation.

The imperial constitution, a modified version of that of the North German Federation, provided for a division of responsibilities between the federal power and the twenty-five states which comprised the Empire. Legislation on federal matters was the task of the Federal Council (*Bundesrat*) and the Parliament (*Reichstag*). Certain constitutional responsibilities were reserved to the Emperor, such as the appointment of the Chancellor, while others were the responsibility of the Emperor and the Federal Council, such as the dissolution of Parliament.

The new state was an arena for new political forces and the resurgence of old ones. Bismarck became embroiled first of all with the Catholic Centre Party, which he perceived as unsympathetic and even disruptive at a time when he wished to safeguard the existence of the new state and build favourable coalitions of parties in the federal and Prussian parliaments. His attacks on the church from 1871 to 1875, involving state control over the clergy, the weakening of church influence in educational matters, compulsory civil marriage, etc., and known as the *Kulturkampf*, were intended to weaken the Centre Party and to assert Bismarck's authority within the Empire. But the centre strengthened its representation despite these anti-Catholic measures of Bismarck, and, especially as the Emperor was not happy about the effects of the *Kulturkampf*, many of the more hostile measures were relaxed or repealed after 1875. The Centre Party remained strong, surviving to be a force in the constellation of parties in the Weimar Republic, while the problems faced by Bismarck of state interference with the churches, especially on educational matters, remain politically sensitive issues even today.

The founding of the Second Empire had coincided with the period of the Paris Commune, whose excesses and anti-authoritarianism offered an awful example to the conservative Bismarck. The accelerating migration to the towns and cities caused by industrial expansion encouraged the spread of socialist ideas in Germany, and these, like political Catholicism, seemed to Bismarck to threaten both the authority of the *Reich* Government and, by an emphasis on internationalism, the national identity of the new state. After making several futile political gestures against socialism and its leaders, Bismarck by 1878 felt compelled to act against the movement more decisively. In that year, following attempts on the Emperor's life, Bismarck was able to force his 'Socialist Laws' through the *Reichstag*, giving him the power to expel socialists from their places of residence, and which banned workers' meetings and also prohibited workers' associations and their publications. All this was implemented with a thoroughness which amounted to police persecution. But, like the *Kulturkampf*, the results were unsatisfactory in relation to Bismarck's purpose. After a temporary check, the votes of the Social Democratic Party increased from nearly 10 per cent in 1884 to almost 20 per cent in 1890.[1] Publications imported from Switzerland and elsewhere enjoyed a clandestine circulation; meetings were held in secret; leaders such as Liebknecht continued courageously to press for socialist reforms and the repeal of discriminatory legislation. Finally, in 1890, the *Reichstag* refused renewal of the laws and the campaign against the socialists ended.

But it was a reforming, not a revolutionary, socialism that developed in Germany in the period before the First World War. The policy of the Government contributed to this, for, alongside the repressive measures which Bismarck introduced against the political freedom of the working class, there was a kind of paternalistic 'state socialism' for their economic welfare: state insurance against sickness, accident insurance, old-age pensions and similar measures. This was one part of the response made by the state to the economic pressures of rapid industrialisation. The other important part was a tariff policy designed to protect the agricultural interests, and which acted as a counterbalance to the industrial cartels that were developing to regulate internal trade.

All these crises of a late-developing nation – the struggles

[1] In 1878 they polled 2½ per cent, and in 1881, 3 per cent.

with the Catholics and the socialists, the problems of the economy – as well as the need to pacify the national minorities now included in the Empire, led Bismarck more and more into the situation of having to bargain with, and to manoeuvre, the parties in the *Reichstag*. Despite his dislike of parties as being against the best interests of the state (a view he shared with a later autocrat, de Gaulle), Bismarck displayed great acumen in balancing National Liberals against Conservatives, Radicals against the Catholic Centre, the national minority parties of Poles and Danes against the ever-present Social Democrats. But all his skill could not disguise his policy of trying to govern without sharing responsibility with the *Reichstag* where he could do so, nor could it hide the fact that this policy was becoming less and less feasible. The death of his old master, William I, in 1888 meant that Bismarck had to look to a new and less sympathetic Kaiser, William II, for support, and soon one of Bismarck's many threats of resignation was taken seriously. Government with the support of the Emperor without Parliament might still have been possible; without the support of either it was impossible.

For the Chancellors who succeeded Bismarck foreign, rather than domestic, issues were the chief concern. The search for colonies led to difficulties in Africa and Asia as well as being the cause of quarrels with Britain and other European states. But it was the search for alliances rather than for colonies, leading as it did to the constellations of the powers that went so readily to war in 1914, that had the most significance for the fate of the Empire and the future course of German politics. Denied an alliance with Britain, who looked on German naval expansion with trepidation, and anxious about the strength of France (who formed an alliance with Russia, posing a two-front threat to Germany), Germany's leaders finally made an alliance with Austria. It was this alliance that drew Germany inexorably into the First World War when the assassination of Archduke Franz Ferdinand involved, in a chain reaction, Serbia, Austria, Russia and Germany, then France, Britain and ultimately America.

During the war itself, the influence of the *Reichstag* in the political system of Germany disappeared almost entirely. They voted the necessary war credits in August 1914, but from then on Germany's domestic politics became inseparable from her military policies, and thus came increasingly under the control of her military leaders. From 1916, indeed, following the appointments of Hindenburg as Chief of the General Staff and Ludendorff as Quartermaster-General, it would not be an exaggeration to call Germany's regime a military dictatorship. Only the unmistakable evidence in October 1918 of Germany's defeat in the field led to the first important abdication – the abandonment by Hindenburg and Ludendorff of their usurped political roles, and their insistence that in the hour of defeat the *Reichstag* and the Chancellor assume political responsibility.

Though this manoeuvre was successful in saving face for the military, and allowed later the myth of the 'stab in the back' of 'an undefeated Army' to gain credence more easily, it was too late to save the Empire. Previously there had been sporadic outbursts of discontent in Germany, as the war and its privations stretched on into a fourth, and then a fifth year, but the sudden news of the pending defeat of what had been so long advertised as an unbeatable military force led to a breakdown of morale, strikes and demonstrations, mutinies and insurrections that rapidly acquired the status of a revolution. Republics were proclaimed in several of the states of the Empire, kings and princes abdicated, the Emperor fled the capital, and on 9 November his abdication was announced from Spa. This was the day on which the German Republic was proclaimed in Berlin, and two days later a German delegation signed the armistice agreement. The war and the Empire ended simultaneously.

THE WEIMAR REPUBLIC

> It is indelibly part of Germany's history that there has never been a successful instance of rebellion or revolution against constituted state authority.[2]

The German revolution of 1918–19 was not an exception to this generalisation. Although a belated attempt at constitutionalism was made in the fortnight between Ludendorff's resignation (26 October 1918) and the proclamation of the

[2] K. de Schweinitz, Jr, *Industrialisation and Democracy* (New York, 1964) p. 161.

Republic in Berlin, the military and the domestic situations permitted it no chance of success. The German revolution which enabled a democratic republic to be established was only filling an already existing vacuum, and did not have as its first task the overthrow of the previous regime. And it was in any case a strange sort of revolution. It lacked any form of central leadership; it was certainly not the result of a Bolshevik conspiracy, for instance. It built up from the mutinies in Wilhelmshaven (28 October) and Kiel (3 November). It was intermingled with spontaneous end-the-war protests by hungry city mobs. It is also difficult to maintain that the revolution had very much to do with creating the new regime, for it was the abdication of the Kaiser and the handing over of governmental power by Prince Max of Baden (the Chancellor) to Ebert and his Socialist Party colleagues that signified the end of the Second Empire and the beginning of the Republic, before the revolution had really got under way.

The first stage of the revolution – the strikes, the demonstrations, the mutinies and the abdications – can be said to have ended with the election in January 1919 of the National Assembly, which was to meet in the town of Weimar (Berlin being too unsettled a city for the task of constitution-drafting), there to settle on a constitution for the new Republic. The second stage, the anti-parliamentary and proletarian revolution termed the 'Spartacist rising', continued until the Government was able to crush it with the aid of its troops. In the process, the leaders of the Spartacists, Rosa Luxemburg and Karl Liebknecht, were killed by soldiers. This dependence of the new regime on the Army mortgaged much of its political credit from the first.

The National Assembly was dominated by the Social Democrats who, with the Independent Socialists, had about 45 per cent of the 421 seats. The Centre Party and the Bavarian Party together sent 20 per cent of the delegates, and the Democratic Party (the successors of the old National Liberals) and the right-wing German National People's Party each had a sizeable representation. By August 1919 they had produced a new constitution which set out the form and the tasks of the new regime and the basic rights and obligations of the citizens. A democratic franchise for both men and women (already used to elect the National Assembly) was used in a system of proportional representation to elect a *Reichstag* for a four-year term. Provision was made for the use of referenda in certain cases. The head of state was to be the President, elected by the people for seven-year terms, and he was to appoint the Chancellor. The Chancellor appointed his own ministers, but the Government was responsible to the *Reichstag*. An important emergency powers clause was also provided. With regard to the states, central authority was increased and the hegemony of Prussia severely restricted. The second chamber in which the states were represented, the *Reichsrat*, had very limited powers.

Before a new legislature could be elected, and the period of provisional government terminated, however, two major problems could not be evaded. Internally, order had to be preserved, and in March 1920 the Kapp *putsch* was only defeated by a general strike in Berlin after the Government had fled the capital. Munich was a centre of disorder and rebellion, and the *Freikorps*, to which many of the former officers and men of the German Army had been attracted, was a potential source of danger to the new Republic. Externally, the terms of the peace treaty had to be settled and accepted.

Richard Watt's excellent account of German politics in the troubled months of 1919 leading up to the signing of the Versailles Treaty concludes: 'It is difficult to consider the events of the period between the armistice and the signing of the Treaty of Versailles as anything but a record of terrible failure.'[3] Responsibility for this failure lies as much with the Allies as with the new Government. Many of the later troubles that led to the downfall of the Weimar Republic were directly caused by the unimaginative and shoddy terms that the Germans were forced to accept at Versailles on 28 June 1919. The internationalism of Wilson, the political acumen of Lloyd George, the shrewdness of Clemenceau were not evidenced in this treaty at all. A few, such as John Maynard Keynes, were more perceptive and realised the dangers this treaty might bring about, but they were not sufficiently influential to revise its major provisions. As for the German delegation, briefed ready for what they anticipated would be unpleasant but at least realistic negotiations with victors who were appreciative of the changes in the regime that had

[3] *The Kings Depart* (London, 1969) p. 501.

occurred in Germany, as well as aware of the problems, their shock on being presented with a dictated peace may be imagined. The German delegation had no alternative but to sign. The terms were harsh indeed: the blame for the war was placed on Germany; her armed forces were limited to the small numbers necessary for internal security; a large reparations burden was imposed; territorial losses were considerable. Many of the more stringent aspects of the treaty were never to be enforced or fulfilled, and it had, after all, been a bloody and bitter war. But there was no encouragement for the new regime in this treaty, and its acceptance could not fail to increase the problems and the internal enemies of the new Republic.

The Weimar Republic, Germany's first working experiment with democratic institutions, lasted just over a dozen years until, in 1933, it was replaced by the most repressive dictatorship in modern history. In those few years it was beset by a series of problems with which it could cope ineffectually, if at all. Political violence was endemic from the first: after the Spartacist rising and the Kapp *putsch*, a series of political assassinations claimed many victims, of whom Erzberger (1921) and Rathenau (1922) were but the two most prominent. Street fighting became a common feature of electoral campaigns long before the critical elections of the early 1930s. Not only were the extremist parties on the left and the right of the 'Weimar Coalition' (Socialists, Democrats and the Centre Party) hostile to the regime in varying degrees but major social institutions were also unable, and – since they had avoided the democratisation process which the formal constitution had undergone – unfitted, to co-operate in more than a neutral fashion. The Army, the Protestant Church, the civil service and the universities were all critical of the Republic. In this context, and lacking a tradition of parliamentary government, the new regime found that the formal constitutional provisions were either too easily circumvented or could be readily adapted to purposes unintended by the framers of the constitution. The uses of the emergency powers under Article 48, the difficulties of forming responsible party Governments, the way in which the critical decisions came to be made in party caucus rather than in parliamentary debate, the ease with which procedural rules could be used as weapons of negativism – these were the political problems which resulted from the constitution itself.

Economic problems prevented Governments from concentrating their efforts towards the correction of the flaws that were appearing in the political structure. A generally uncooperative attitude by the German Government over reparation payments led the French to seize on defaults in payments as an excuse for the occupation of the Ruhr in 1923. Passive resistance, terrorism and French repression worsened the situation. The occupation coincided with, and interacted with, a rapid inflation of the currency which hit at most classes of the population but which had most impact, in terms of political effect, on the middle classes, turning their lukewarm acceptance of the regime into at best apathy, at worst a receptiveness to nationalist and extremist panaceas. Only a timely combination of currency reform, a change of Government in Germany and France which allowed both to take a more sensible view of the reparations problem, and the beginning of economic recovery stimulated by foreign investment allowed the Republic to survive this period of crisis. But the economy remained brittle, susceptible to any adverse changes in patterns of world trade, and when the international depression commenced in 1929 Germany was one of the worst affected of the major economies. Unemployment soared; wages plummeted. Bitter arguments over supplementary unemployment payments as the insurance-based funds were exhausted poisoned the political atmosphere. And as the depression worsened, so the extremist parties, the Communists and the Nazis, gained votes, members, financial support and confidence.

Few politicians, certainly few German politicians, believed that 1918 had marked the end of European warfare even for their own lifetimes. Uneasiness over frontiers, the remaining international controls over German affairs under the Treaty of Versailles, unsettled disputes concerning national minorities, the lack of confidence in the system of collective security offered by the new League of Nations were all factors which prompted successive German Governments to practise as assiduously as their nineteenth-century predecessors the old diplomacy of alliances, pacts and treaties. Notice of these intentions was served by the signing of the Rapallo Treaty (1922) with the Soviet Union, and, after the Ruhr occupation had ended, Germany negotiated the Locarno Treaty (1925) with France, Britain, Belgium and Italy by which the frontiers of 1919 were guaranteed, and Germany was permitted to enter the League of Nations. Relations with America were mainly concerned with plans for easing the reparations problem. The last of these was the Young Plan (1929) which proposed spreading payments over a fifty-nine-year period and had certain safeguards built into the plan in Germany's favour. But first the onset of the depression, then Hitler's rise to power, nullified operation of the plan.

THE DECLINE OF THE WEIMAR REPUBLIC

The Weimar Republic ended because of the political events between the appointment of Brüning as Chancellor in 1930 and the appointment of Hitler to the same office in 1933. But although the pattern of events answers the question of 'how?', the question of 'why?' is more significant, more complex and less easy to answer.

The economic crisis produced by the international depression led to political difficulties in 1930. Brüning, of the Centre Party, was appointed Chancellor when the governing coalition of Social Democrats, the People's Party and the Centre Party split over the question of unemployment benefits. Unable to command a majority in the *Reichstag*, Brüning became increasingly dependent on the support of President Hindenburg. Frequent use was made of the emergency powers under Article 48 of the constitution. In the election of September 1930 the extremist parties made gains, the Nazi Party increasing their seats from a dozen to 107 in a bitterly fought campaign in which all the parties pressed for revisions of the Versailles Treaty. For over two years, coping with a series of economic and political problems, Brüning survived as Chancellor. In 1932 Hindenburg was re-elected as President, though requiring a second ballot against Hitler before gaining the necessary absolute majority. But now being more than ever under the influence of his right-wing nationalist associates, the ageing President dismissed Brüning only a few weeks after the presidential election. In this way Hindenburg 'murdered not only the German Republic, but also the peace of all Europe'.[4]

[4] E. Eyck, *A History of the Weimar Republic*, vol. II (London, 1964) p. 392.

A Government of Berlin 'gentlemen', with von Papen as Chancellor, replaced that of Brüning. An election followed shortly afterwards, in July 1932, in which the Nazis became the second party in the *Reichstag*, with 230 seats. Papen was unable to find a majority in the new *Reichstag*, secured a dissolution and another election was held in November. This time the tide turned somewhat against the Nazis, but Papen could not find a majority even so, and was replaced by Schleicher. The new Chancellor tried to bring in the Nazis on a subordinate basis into the Government. Hitler gambled. He refused to join any Government except as Chancellor. After some eight weeks of office Schleicher resigned, and Hindenburg, the Field-Marshal of the world war years, appointed Hitler, an ex-corporal, as Chancellor. 'The attempt by the German people to rule themselves had failed. A time now came when Germany ceased to be a state based on law.'[5]

But why was the Weimar Republic so easily destroyed? What caused this 'attempt by the German people to rule themselves' to fail? No simple, single-factor explanation seems adequate, partly because there are so very many to choose from, partly because they tend to lack conviction when they are rigorously examined.

Economic explanations, concerned with the depression or the 'internal contradictions of capitalism', leave unanswered the question of why Germany should have succumbed to authoritarianism, but not the United States, France, Britain or Austria, all of which nations were also beset by economic difficulties. Constitutional explanations stress the emergency powers article and its misuse or over-use, or the proportional voting system which was associated with splinter parties and unstable coalitions. But these were at the most symptoms of troubles rather than causes. There was a continuing emergency from 1929 onwards, and one reason for it was the depth of the political divisions among the German people. To blame the electoral system for creating those divisions is illogical, for they existed in similar form in the multi-party but non-proportional parliaments of the pre-war period. The fact is that, under any electoral system whatever, it would have been impossible by 1930 to find a responsible governing majority and a constructive opposition. Political explanations

[5] Ibid., p. 486.

tend to stress the Versailles Treaty as a time-bomb that had to explode, or the friction between the parties of the extreme left and the extreme right. Yet harsh treaties (including those imposed by a victorious Germany at Frankfurt in 1871 and Brest-Litovsk in 1918) have not always led to severe domestic political strife, nor did every state with extremist parties at each other's throats find itself dominated by a Hitler in the end.

A more convincing answer must be one that takes all these factors into account as constituting a conjunction of special import in the Germany of 1930–3, and must also look to the underlying situation that made these factors so significant in Germany then.

The economic and political crisis in Germany from 1930 onwards thus presented to the enemies of the Republic the opportunity to bring about its overthrow. For the conservatives and the monarchists surrounding Hindenburg, for the industrialists such as Thyssen and Krupp, the generals such as Schleicher, this could be done, they imagined, by converting a democratic parliamentary regime into an authoritarian presidential system, if necessary by means of short-term collaboration with Hitler and the Nazis. For the extremist parties of the left and the right, allied at the very least in their hatred of the moderate elements in politics and their readiness to seek populist, even revolutionary, solutions,[6] the crisis could be exploited in several ways. The left could blame capitalism and international finance; the right could revive slogans about Versailles, the 'criminals of November' and the 'stab in the back'.[7] But America, France and Britain were all faced with economic crisis and waxing political extremism in this period, yet their political systems survived intact, if not unaffected, and in Germany this unpropitious constellation of economic and political troubles would still not have been sufficient to bring about the Nazi dictatorship had there not existed underlying weaknesses in the social system.

[6] See the article by A. Ascher and G. Lewy, 'National Bolshevism in Weimar Germany', *Social Research*, XXIII 4 (winter 1956) 450–80.

[7] This was a legend which grew out of the circumstances in which the war came to an end in 1918, and the evasion of responsibilities by the generals in sending civilians to sign the armistice. Later the claim was made that the German Army had not been defeated in the field but 'stabbed in the back' by revolutionaries at home.

'However one turns the problem, therefore, its solution must be sought in the structures of German society.'[8] Professor Dahrendorf has summarised the flawed social structure of Weimar Germany in terms of three major features. First, despite the formal constitutional changes marking the transition from monarchy to democratic republic, there was little real change underneath. The elites in particular were a major continuity, in terms of personnel (the civil servants, the officers, the industrial and educational leaders) and their anti-democratic attitudes. The politicians, afforded greater formal powers by the new constitution than under the Empire, lacked experience in the exercise of responsibility, and all too frequently had to demonstrate their reliance on the 'old guard' – in the case of the military, to put down internal disorder, in the civil service for the administration of complex policies, in the diplomatic service for negotiations with suspicious foreign powers, and in the end reliance on the commander-in-chief of the old guard himself, Hindenburg, to rule whenever the *Reichstag* prevented the Government from governing. Secondly, the population never acquired democatic patterns of political behaviour. The social role of the citizen had traditionally been passive, non-participatory, and so it remained under Weimar. They would vote, yes (turnout in national elections was generally around 75–80 per cent), but as a social duty. Otherwise the home was considered to be the proper arena of the citizen, not the meeting-hall or the party office. If things were going wrong, it was up to 'them' to put things right if they could. Thirdly, there was an aversion towards regarding politics as a proper method for dealing with conflict, an aversion that made acceptable government by decree, whether by Hindenburg or Hitler. The election slogan of Hindenburg's presidential campaign in 1932 sums this up: 'With him! Germans, for once put aside all your divisions.'

So Weimar was never a viable democracy. Without the opportunism of the Nazis, without the opportunities offered them by the depression, the social system might have adapted gradually and the political system have been preserved. But the strains were severe, as were to be the consequences.

[8] R. Dahrendorf, *Society and Democracy in Germany* (London, 1968) p. 387.

2 The Nazi Revolution and the Second World War

THE NAZI REVOLUTION

Hitler came to power constitutionally. The Nazi Party had become the second largest party in the state under the Weimar electoral system. Even the dictatorial powers acquired by Hitler were, initially, acquired by adherence to democratic forms. Yet for all this, the Weimar Republic really ended its existence the day Hitler became Chancellor, and the activities of Hitler and his supporters from then onward amounted to a political revolution.

The Nazi Party was formed in 1920 from a miscellaneous collection of right-wing groups, and was influenced in its early years by the successes of the Italian Fascists who seized power in 1922. The party met with only small success in its early years, and in 1923 Hitler was tempted into seeking the overthrow of the Bavarian Government by means of a *putsch*, in company with certain elements of the armed forces, Ludendorff and other reactionaries. The failure of this *coup* led to a short prison sentence for Hitler (during which he commenced his book *Mein Kampf*) and organisational disruption for the party, faced as it was with competition from other right-wing nationalist parties. The growing stability of the Government and economic recovery reduced the political attraction of the Nazis, and only the opportunities offered by the referendum on the Young Plan for reparations (1929) and the economic crisis of 1930 allowed the Nazis to create a national reputation (though in certain localities in, e.g., Bavaria and Schleswig-Holstein they met with especially substantial success).

The ideology of the party was a mixture of nationalism, anti-Semitism, demands for strong and centralised government, the repeal of the Versailles Treaty and a vague catalogue of social reforms directed at 'the establishment' and big business. Within the party itself there were various quarrels over the 'nationalist' and the 'socialist' emphases within

National Socialism, but with the ascendancy of Hitler a flexibility of ideology was introduced that enabled the party to appear as the champion of the masses as well as the protector of private enterprise against Bolshevism, the defender of the small business owner and the farmer, as well as the ally of the Army and the repository of national tradition. Only the thread of anti-Semitism was continuous, for this was the theme that could best appeal to the disgruntled of all classes, and could gloss over the otherwise contradictory appeals to the various segments of the electorate which Hitler sought to attract.[1]

The methods by which the party campaigned grew more and more ruthless. The para-military auxiliary groups, especially the SA (*Sturmabteilung*) in its brown uniform, developed a reputation for street violence that became a characteristic of German election campaigns, especially in the period from 1930 to 1933.[2] For a while in 1932 the SA was banned by Hindenburg, but this ban was revoked after a few weeks.

But no political party could survive for long without financial resources – the Nazis, with their extravagant auxiliaries and functionaries on the payroll, least of all. By a stroke of fortune, the campaign to defeat the Young Plan in 1929 led the Nationalist Party leader, Hugenberg, to form a group of representatives of right-wing organisations to concert a strategy. This group included Hitler, and the Nazis became the chief beneficiaries of the large subventions received then and later from industrialists such as Duisberg, of IG Farben, and Thyssen, who later joined the party itself. By 1932 even the patrician Gustav Krupp was contributing heavily, despite his reservations about the distasteful political style of Hitler.[3]

Hitler's Cabinet in 1933 was a coalition, in which his party had initially but two other representatives: Göring (without portfolio) and Frick (Interior). But it was a Cabinet that could be expected to sympathise with right-wing measures, including as it did such personalities as Hugenberg (Economics Minister), von Papen (Vice-Chancellor), von Neurath

[1] See M. Needler, 'Hitler's Anti-Semitism: A Political Appraisal', *Public Opinion Quarterly*, XXIV 4 (winter 1960) 665–9.

[2] The way the party obtained power at the local level, by parades, propaganda, coercion and compromise, has been tellingly described in W. S. Allen, *The Nazi Seizure of Power* (London, 1966).

[3] W. Manchester, *The Arms of Krupp* (London, 1969) pp. 400–8.

(Foreign Minister) and von Blomberg (Defence). However, Hitler could not find the parliamentary majority which had been Hindenburg's self-justification for agreeing to accept Hitler as Chancellor, so an election was called (the eighth national campaign since 1928[4]). The Nazi campaign was more vicious in its style and more anti-democratic in its content than ever before. The mysterious burning of the *Reichstag* in the middle of the campaign gave Hitler additional excuse for attacking the Communists, who were blamed for the fire, and for excluding them from the *Reichstag* after the election itself. The Nazis polled 44 per cent of the votes, enough with the votes of the Nationalists to secure a narrow majority, and even, with the aid of the Centre Party and the absence of the Communists, to secure an amendment to the constitution. This took the form of an Enabling Act, passed in an atmosphere of Nazi intimidation by 441 votes to 94. This Act was the cornerstone of the edifice of tyranny which Hitler now constructed, for it gave the Government powers to legislate without the *Reichstag*, and regardless of the stipulations of the Weimar constitution.

Such powers were used in particular to consolidate the hold of the Nazi Party on the German state, to give the Nazis their position of monopoly as the only legal party, and to turn German society into a monolithic and totalitarian culture. After the Communist Party, the Social Democratic Party became the target, and then the Centre, Nationalist, People's, Bavarian and Democratic parties dissolved themselves following attacks on their premises, threats and other forms of coercion. Almost superfluously, Hitler signed a decree in July 1933 announcing that the Nazi Party was henceforth to be the only legal party in Germany. In case the states of Germany (especially Prussia) should constitute an independent threat, their powers were transferred to the central Government in 1934. The trade union movement became absorbed in the Labour Front; the mass media were put under governmental control; even the churches were intimidated and infiltrated. This process of *Gleichschaltung* ('co-ordination') was the real German revolution. Its result was the merging of state and party, and

[4] The eight were: the general elections of 1928, 1930, 1932 (twice) and 1933; the two presidential election campaigns of 1932; and the referendum on the Young Plan in 1929.

the dictatorship of Hitler through the party as his instrument, and the support of a coercive apparatus of terrorism, concentration camps and executions, unhindered by the now-abolished rule of law.

The new Government did not rely entirely on such negative measures. It needed to retain the support of the people who had voted for it in the elections of 1932 and 1933, and, as far as possible, to keep the rest of the population quiescent by measures that would alleviate the widespread and persistent economic distress that had given the Nazis their opportunity of power, and promote some degree of positive attachment to the Government by an aggressive nationalism. A programme of public works, labour camps, conscription and rearmament revived the economy. The concentration of industry was encouraged as a reward to the big industrialists who had helped to finance the party, but was nevertheless accompanied by a growing number of restrictions on profits, investment policies and managerial discretion generally. Agriculture also received attention, but here, too, assistance was only obtained by the farmer along with increasing state intervention in marketing policies, land ownership and land use.

THE NAZI LEADERSHIP

Three elements of the Nazi leadership are of particular relevance in considering how Germany became a dictatorship, and together they explain much about the progress of Germany towards the disasters of the Second World War and the occupation by the victors of a devastated land. These elements were the personality of Hitler himself, the Nazi elite and its characteristics, and the relationship of the military towards the political developments that occurred.

Hitler's personality had many interesting facets, but certain of these can be highlighted as of special significance for the politics of Germany between 1933 and 1945. The early life of Hitler was full of frustrations and insecurities, and his adult personality came to reflect these. His war-time experiences, his early contacts with the extremist political groups of the post-1918 years, his attempted *coup* in Munich further shaped his attitudes and ideas. His imprisonment following the *coup*, in 1923–4, gave him the opportunity to put his philosophy into a book, a work which reflects many of his strengths and weaknesses of personality. Of the many aspects of this personality that could be cited, his imagination and lack of realism, his personal charm and his ability to overawe, his genius as a speaker and his self-confidence as a leader add up to an almost classic example of the charismatic leader. The German people came to expect the extraordinary from him, and he came increasingly to believe that he could perform the extraordinary. The many memoirs and chronicles of the Nazi era bear witness to the unconventional political and military skills of Hitler, and particularly how he was able to convince all sorts of doubters against their better judgement. But his lack of attachment to the real world, which was the negative side of his charisma, became increasingly important for Germany as the war progressed. To all this must be added a lust for power that has rarely been matched in modern history. Absolute power corrupts absolutely, but the search for such power has much to do with the ability to be corrupted by it.

The characteristics of the Nazi elite are of interest in understanding how the party came to power, and what it used that power for. Although monolithic in its obedience to the *Führer,* organisationally it was divided into several overlapping sub-elites. The SA was eliminated as a sub-elite in the 'night of the long knives' (30 June 1934), but there remained the party bureaucracy itself, led first by Hess, then by Bormann; Himmler's SS (*Schutzstaffel*); the propaganda organisation of Goebbels; the state apparatus in which figures such as Ribbentrop were important; and military and economic influentials such as Göring and Speer. These were all permitted to formulate the policy alternatives from which Hitler could select or not as he pleased. They all had some access to him for special needs from time to time, and all were used for his own special purposes. This mosaic of petty empires was a quite deliberate development on the part of Hitler. The personal jealousies it gave rise to were sufficient safeguard against any organisation-based challenge to his own authority.

The other interesting feature is the composition of the Nazi elite. A study by Daniel Lerner and his associates[5] has demonstrated that the Nazi leaders were not only different from the general population but in significant ways from their own

[5] D. Lerner *et al.*, 'The Nazi Elite', in *World Revolutionary Elites*, ed. H. Lasswell and D. Lerner (Cambridge, Mass., 1965) chap. 5.

rank-and-file as well. They tended to be younger than is usual for leadership on such a scale; they often had a background of occupational and educational instability; many were 'frustrated intellectuals'; often they were of humble origin but eager to seize the opportunities offered by the party's success to gain social prestige. Above all, they tended to be 'marginal men', with unusual qualities, originating from places like Austria (e.g. Hitler himself), Bavaria (where the party was formed) or the 'lost territories' of the East (e.g. Rosenberg), and often possessing foreign associations through marriage or education, for instance. Like the social and psychological background of Hitler himself, these characteristics are illuminating in the search for an understanding of the Nazi cataclysm.

A revolution, to be complete, requires a substitution of leadership. The political leadership of the Weimar Republic had been defeated with its own weapons of constitutionalism. There remained, however, the Army whose presence had cast a shadow over the political events of 1930–3. Hitler had always been aware of the political importance of the Army; his experiences in the *coup* of 1923, his observations of their influence on the actions of the Weimar politicians, his knowledge of their concurrence in his own nomination as Chancellor were cause enough for such awareness. The threat of a *coup*, never absent from the political scene before 1933, was not likely to become less now that Hitler had assumed power. Hitler therefore took steps to win over the Army by promises of rearmament, flattery of the generals, the restoration of old privileges and the removal of the competitive threat of the SA. Later, from a position of more strength, he proceeded to purge the Army of its independent elements and replaced them with Nazis, took the position of Commander-in-Chief himself, and turned the Army's own code of honour on itself by requiring the generals to swear an oath of loyalty to Hitler personally.

THE NAZI STATE

With quite deliberate purpose, the Nazi leadership tried to use their political dominance to make profound changes in German life. Though, like the Bolsheviks, and the republicans in Germany in 1919, they found they had to compromise with the establishment in order to provide the administrative skills which could not be produced from their own ranks, this was countered by a process of Nazification of the civil service, the local government system, the judiciary and any other social institution regarded as being important in the new state. Much of the increase in party membership came from officials anxious to safeguard their jobs, though many in any case joined quite voluntarily. But the remarkable continuity in personnel in these major institutions from the days of the Empire, through the Weimar period, into the 'Thousand-Year *Reich*', is a notable feature of German politics in the pre-1945 period.

Alongside the political revolution there were revolutionary changes in society and culture in Germany under the Nazis, fostered deliberately in conformity with Hitler's ideas about the 'new Germany' he wished to create. Echoes of the Norse legends, an emphasis on physical activities for leisure, concepts of 'blood and soil' and the superiority of the rural life were underpinned by the fundamental notion of Aryan racial superiority.

Socially, the Third *Reich* was effective in destroying many of the traditional features of German life, which had persisted relatively unaltered into the Weimar years. Rather immobile patterns of status, associated with hierarchies of social class and occupation (especially in the Army and the civil service), were modified considerably. Party membership became an important cross-cutting factor; the multiplicity of party organisations added to the uncertainty. Some of the changes that occurred had been apparent to a smaller extent under Weimar, and were as much a function of industrialisation and, later, war itself as of deliberate Nazi policy, but the speed and penetration of such changes owed much to the negative attitudes of the Nazi leadership towards the 'establishment' of the pre-revolutionary past.

Of all the forces making for change within the new order, propaganda through the mass media was the most pervasive and the most significant, for it served indiscriminately the various other agencies of change which came into existence. Under Goebbels' control, the Press and the radio, the cinema, posters and banners, rallies and parades – everything that could carry a slogan, embody a symbol or convey a message –

was used to persuade or to intimidate as necessary. In this way the public was mobilised to give not just passive support but active assistance, whether it was for economic changes introduced by the Government, the aggressive foreign policy that promised to undo the humiliations of Versailles, or finally for the prosecution of the 'total war' that this foreign policy made necessary.

THE ROAD TO DEFEAT

Apart from anti-Semitism and hatred of democratic political forms and ideals, the theme most frequently repeated in Hitler's rhetoric before and after his appointment as Chancellor was the need for Germany to 'rectify' the provisions of the Versailles Treaty concerning territorial losses. Once in power, Hitler produced a chain of policies which led from the remilitarisation of the Rhineland to his own suicide in the ruins of an occupied Berlin. Each link in that chain was justified by Hitler in terms of the compulsive logic of Nazi ideology, from the right of Germany to sovereignty in what was, after all, admittedly still German territory (the Rhineland), the need for Germanic peoples to be united with the *Reich* (Austria, the Sudetenland, Danzig), to the destiny of the superior German race to conquer and rule the inferior *Untermenschen*, the Slavonic peoples of the East.

Following the death of Hindenburg (1934), Hitler increased his freedom of action by assuming the Presidency as well as being Chancellor. In 1935, following a plebiscite, the Saar returned to Germany, and in 1936, after a campaign of denunciation of unfair treaties, Hitler sent troops marching into the demilitarised Rhineland zone, in defiance of the Versailles Treaty. Formal diplomatic protests from France and Britain were the only sanctions that resulted, and Hitler continued the more confidently with his programme of rearmament, extending the term of compulsory military service, the strengthening of ties with Italy and Japan, and interference in the Spanish Civil War to provide his pilots with experience and his adversaries with problems. In 1938 German troops entered Austria in the name of the *Anschluss* (union) with Germany, and the complaints of ill-treatment fostered by the Nazis' allies among the Sudetenland Germans in Czechoslovakia led to a crisis which was resolved by the

Munich Conference in September 1938, at which Germany, Italy, France and Britain agreed that Germany should occupy the Sudetenland. Poland seemed to be the next victim, especially in view of the importance paid by Hitler to the Danzig question, and this was made even more certain by the sudden conclusion of a non-aggression pact between Russia and Germany in August 1939, which removed the likelihood of Russia joining Poland's guarantors, France and Britain, should those Western powers go to Poland's aid by declaring war on Germany.

> BERLIN, September 3
>
> Hitler's 'counter-attack' on Poland has on this Sabbath day become a world war.[6]

The Western powers, France and Britain, had acquiesced in the expansionist policies of Hitler partly because of their own unreadiness for war, partly from a fond belief in Hitler's promise after every advance that 'this will be my last territorial demand'. The invasion of Poland could not go unchallenged, if the credibility of the foreign policies of either country was to be preserved, and if there was to be any chance of limiting Germany's expansion in Europe. An ultimatum to Hitler was ignored. War was declared. Shirer goes on to describe the reactions of the German people to loudspeaker announcements of England's declaration of war:

> When it was finished, there was not a murmur. They just stood there as they were before. Stunned. The people cannot realise yet that Hitler has led them into a world war.[7]

This realisation was not to be long delayed. Following a year of German successes, the ejection of British troops from the Continent, the fall of France, the attack on Russia in defiance of the 1939 pact, the bombs began to fall on German cities, the German armies were first stopped, then pushed back; the Americans entered the war and, accompanying all this, Germany became increasingly like an armed camp. More and more controls were introduced, over the economy, the workplace, the home. The concentration camps of pre-war years expanded and multiplied. The policy of eliminating the Jew-

[6] W. Shirer, *Berlin Diary* (London, n.d. [1941]) p. 161.
[7] Ibid.

ish populations of German and German-occupied territories added a further grim tone to daily life. The *Gestapo*, the informant, the blockwarden were instruments of internal terror.

Attempts at resistance were made. Some of these, such as the activities of the Scholls' 'White Rose' group in Munich, had no conceivable hope of being more than a symbol for the future. Others were more promising, particularly the plans developed by a circle of civic and military figures which resulted in the '20 July plot' in 1944, when von Stauffenberg succeeded in planting a bomb during a conference at which Hitler was present. By a combination of accidents, the bomb failed to kill Hitler, the *coup* which was to follow the assassination was defeated in its earliest stages, and the enraged Hitler ordered a series of revengeful executions. The invading armies continued their two-front advance, and finally Hitler committed suicide, leaving his successors to surrender in May 1945.

The 'Thousand-Year *Reich*' had lasted twelve years. In that time it changed the history of Europe, but its effects on Germany itself were the most far-reaching. The state which Bismarck had unified was divided. The territory which Hitler had ruled was governed by occupational forces. The tyranny of a totalitarian dictator was replaced, in West Germany, four years after its end by a self-conscious democracy that, more than twenty years after its foundation, is stronger than ever. Yet Hitler's attack on the past had been thorough. The Third *Reich* was not just a different political regime; it was Germany's 'modernisation revolution'.[8] Society in Germany today, in its cultural as well as its political aspects, is different from German society before, as well as during, Hitler's period of rule. The Nazi state had represented an irreversible break with the past.

[8] See Dahrendorf, *Society and Democracy in Germany*, chap. 25.

3 Reconstruction and Reconstitution, 1945–69

SURRENDER, OCCUPATION AND RECONSTRUCTION

Germany was defeated in May 1945 by an alliance of British, American and Russian armies. Unlike the experience of 1918, when the sudden collapse of the German armies found the Allies politically unprepared, conferences at Quebec and Yalta had laid the basis for a division of Germany into zones of occupation, from which reparations were to be extracted (principally to benefit Russia) and where de-Nazification was to be carried out, though more extreme policies involving the dismemberment of Germany, and the Morgenthau Plan to make Germany a pastoral economy, were not proceeded with. Occupation policies were activated as the armies advanced into Germany and, following the surrender and arrest of the nominal successor Government headed by Admiral Dönitz, the occupation regime was established as the new Government of Germany.

The problems facing the occupying powers were grave. Germany lay in ruins. Homes, factories, offices, railways, waterworks, hospitals were rubble. The administrative structure had collapsed. Refugees flocked westward, escaping the Russians. Medical and communications facilities were desperately short. And the people were starving. The Potsdam Conference (July–August 1945) attempted with some success to provide a co-ordinated policy for the four zones of occupation (France had been given a zone from the British and American zones) and Berlin (occupied by all four powers). Concrete results did emerge: over war-crimes trials to be held at Nürnberg, over demilitarisation and de-Nazification, the reintroduction of civil rights, the re-establishment of a judicial system and local government, for example. But already disagreements – which Hitler had hoped would save his collapsing regime in 1944–5 – were now appearing in the peace-time relations between Russia and the Western Allies.

These disagreements showed up most rapidly over Berlin. The city as a whole was governed by a four-power council, but each of the Allies administered a separate zone. In 1946 elections were held for the municipal council, but the Communists (using the title of Socialist Unity Party – SED), despite considerable propaganda efforts and intimidatory tactics, were badly defeated,[1] and no other election in Berlin as a whole was ever held. The determination of the Russians to spread Communism in their own zone of occupation and in Berlin led to intensification of disagreement over such matters as reparations policies, inter-zonal communication and the future of Germany as a state. The Marshall Plan (1947), and the creation in the American and British zones of a bizonal economic authority (1947), which in 1948 took on wider legislative and executive functions, further incensed Russia. The introduction of currency reform in 1948, as a means of stimulating the economy and preventing Russian abuse of the occupation currency system, led to the 'Berlin Blockade'. This was an attempt by the Russians to put pressure on the Western powers and the Berliners by closing road, rail and water access-routes from the west, which passed through Russian-occupied territory. The response was a massive airlift operation of supplies to Berlin, and Berlin itself became divided, like Germany, into a western and eastern sector. This rift between the Russians and the Western powers hastened the creation of two separate states in Germany.

Meanwhile in the Western zones the occupation Governments encouraged the re-establishment of self-government first at the local, then at the *Land*, level. In the American zone, for instance, local elections were held as early as January 1946, and in June of that year constitutional conventions were elected for the four *Länder* of the zone: Bremen, Bavaria, Baden-Württemberg and Hesse. The constitutions were ratified in the same year by the Americans subject to certain reserved powers and a limited veto, and *Land* self-government was a reality by 1947. In the British zone a similar development occurred, though at a slower pace; unlike the Americans, Britain was in any case less ready to encourage

[1] Result: SPD 49 per cent, CDU 22 per cent, SED 20 per cent, Liberals 9 per cent.

regional, as opposed to national, loyalties. The first *Land* elections in the British zone took place in April 1947. France, for reasons of security and self-interest, showed no willingness to encourage German self-government, until growing East–West divisions forced her to co-operate with the American and British authorities in 1948.

The development of self-government could not very well proceed without representative political organisations and media of political communication. As a check on the possible re-emergence of anti-democratic influences, the occupation authorities instituted a system of licensing of parties and the Press which permitted a suitable structural basis to form for the reintroduction of democratic politics.

The process of creating a viable and democratic system of self-government for Germany as a whole was a more difficult, and in any case considered to be a longer-term, undertaking. The famous Stuttgart speech of the American Secretary of State, Byrnes, in 1946, had emphasised to an audience of German and Allied officials the determination of the Americans not to leave Germany until it was a democratic free state again. But the intransigent attitude of the Russians, and the successes of local self-government and the bizonal structures in the British and American occupation areas, led these countries to consider very seriously the possibility of creating a provisional West German state independent of Russian wishes or co-operation. A conference was held in London in 1948, at which representatives of Britain, the United States, France and the Benelux countries agreed on the desirability of a federal and democratic West German state. To this end, and after conferring with the various Ministers-President of the *Länder*, the authorities decided that a Parliamentary Council should be elected from the *Länder* to draft a constitution. The party composition of the 65-member Council,[2] elected in August 1948, was: Christian Democrats (Christian Socialists in Bavaria) 27, Social Democrats 27, Liberals 5, other parties 6.

The result of the deliberations of the Parliamentary Council was the Basic Law which was promulgated on 23 May 1949. The eight months of these deliberations were filled with political manoeuvres, the consideration of competing

[2] Five observers from West Berlin were also to be present.

schemes, the clash of opposing interests, and the conclusion of as many important compromises as at the Philadelphia Convention in 1787. While the political parties were the most coherent of the voices to be heard, others were of considerable importance. Not the least of these was Germany's own past. The mistakes of the Weimar period and the disasters of Nazism were to be avoided at all costs, by the use of a different electoral system, the constructive vote of no confidence, the weak position of the President and the strength of the federal system. The Allies were another important influence, and the Basic Law clearly imitates the compelling models of American federation and British parliamentary-based responsible government, for instance. The *Länder* were interested in states' rights, in preserving their existing and wide-ranging powers within the new state structure. The churches, the unions and the local government organisations were all concerned with the outcome of specific sections of the draft constitutional proposals.

The Basic Law itself was approved by the occupation authorities in May 1949, though the Allies reserved certain powers over such matters as Berlin and the occupation itself. Then it was submitted to the several *Land* parliaments for ratification. All but Bavaria voted in favour (of 1,234 *Landtag* members, 874 voted in favour of ratification, 236 against, and the rest abstained or were absent). Bavaria wanted more autonomy than the Basic Law offered, or even confederate status, and its *Landtag* rejected ratification by 101 votes to 63, but realistically agreed in a second vote to consider it as binding on Bavaria if it was ratified by two-thirds of the *Länder*, as required by Article 144 of the Basic Law. This being achieved, the first parliamentary elections for the new Republic took place in August 1949.

Nearly 80 per cent of the electorate voted in that first election, and the mixture of direct and proportional electoral systems gave the Christian Democrats (CDU), with their Bavarian sister-party, the Christian Socialists (CSU), 139 seats to the Social Democrats' (SPD) 131. The Free Democrats obtained 52 seats, and no fewer than eight other parties shared the remaining 80 seats, the Communists (15) and the right-wing German and Bavarian parties (each 17 seats) being the largest of these. The Liberal, Theodor Heuss, was elected as the Republic's first President. Then, on the nomination of Heuss, the leader of the CDU, Konrad Adenauer, was elected Chancellor by the *Bundestag* (though only by a margin of one vote). Despite earlier talk of a 'Grand Coalition' with the SPD, which had come to naught mainly because of the opposition of Schumacher (the SPD leader), a coalition was formed between the CDU–CSU, the FDP and the German Party (DP).

THE ADENAUER PERIOD

The Adenauer 'era' lasted from his election as Chancellor in September 1949 to his resignation in October 1963. His period in office would in any case have been important for the future development of the new state. Adenauer made certain that it was crucial. His policies, his political style and his political attitudes shaped the Germany of 1971 as Bismarck had shaped the Germany that came into existence in 1871.

He came to the Chancellorship at the late age of seventy-three, already very much the elder statesman of his party, with long experience as *Oberbürgermeister* of Köln and, in his capacity as President of the Parliamentary Council, having been very influential in the shaping of the Basic Law. His political background was untainted by Nazism, but equally it was clear that he was not likely to be sympathetic to Communism.

His first task was the economic and social reconstruction of his country. Social security legislation was introduced, with benefits related to the cost of living. Legislation for the equalisation of the financial burdens imposed by the war and for compensation for victims of Nazism was a sign of good faith for those dubious about the swift re-establishment of an independent German state, though nominally a democratic one. Erhard, the Minister of Economics, built on the foundations of the 1948 currency reform and the Marshall Plan what he termed a 'social-market economy', so successfully, indeed, that within a few years the phrase 'economic miracle' (*Wirtschaftswunder*) was being used to describe the growth in the economy, stimulated as it was by intensive investment in modern equipment to replace plant destroyed in the war or removed for reparations, helped by low expenditure on defence and the export boom caused by the Korean War. The trade unions were carefully courted by Adenauer's Government, and strikes were rare despite the long working hours that were necessary. Education was fostered, though it remained in many ways one of the more conservative and tradition-bound areas of German social life. But, encouraged by British and American pressures, a deliberate element of 'education for democracy' was introduced, countering tendencies to gloss over or distort Germany's own past. These policies were generally successful in the rehabilitation of Germany, and the elections of 1953, 1957 and 1961 were all victories for the CDU–CSU. Indeed, in 1957 the CDU–CSU won 270 seats in a *Bundestag* of 497 members, but nevertheless formed a coalition Government. Meanwhile revisions of the electoral law and polarisation of the electorate meant that by 1961 only the Christian Union parties, the Social Democrats and the Free Democrats were still represented in the *Bundestag*.

The period of Adenauer's Chancellorship was not without its difficulties and crises. Apart from the foreign policy problems arising out of the pivotal position of West Germany in a divided Europe, and the continuing concern of the Western powers, there were the problems of overcoming the Nazi past, coping with the refugees, and generally protecting an insecure democracy against various anti-democratic tendencies.

The determination to overcome the Nazi past involved special reparations payments to Israel, severe penalties for anti-Semitic activities (though, with a much diminished Jewish population, opportunities for such activities were lessened), and the continuation of prosecutions of war criminals, despite growing feelings among some sections of German society that a time limit should be enforced for such prosecutions. Adenauer was aware of foreign sensitivity on the issue of war criminals, and the dangers of a re-emergence of Nazism, but was very ready to accept former Nazis in high governmental posts if he considered he could have confidence in them. This led to several protests against the appointment of men such as Globke in the Chancellor's Department, and Oberländer as Minister for All-German Affairs. The refugees were also a problem from the first. Regarded by the westerners as rivals for scarce housing, welfare and jobs, and themselves resentful because of the circumstances that had forced them to leave their own regions, the refugees were not easily assimilated into West German society. Added to this, they held rallies and formed organisations to preserve their cultural identities and put pressure on the Government for reunification of Germany. Their own Refugees Party, the BHE (*Bund der Heimatsvertriebenen und Entrechteten* – League of Expellees and those Deprived of Rights) was an important factor in Bonn politics. But economic recovery, the growing permanence of East–West divisions in Europe and Adenauer's strategy of giving the party seats in his 1953 Government reduced the political importance of the BHE as a party, though the refugees remained a significant pressure-group.

Fears of the revival of political extremism led the Government to bring cases before the Constitutional Court for the prohibition of the right-wing Socialist Reich Party (SRP), banned in 1952, and the Communist Party (KPD), banned in 1956. These bans were imposed in accordance with Article 21 of the Basic Law, though not without some criticism of the Government's wisdom in initiating such proceedings. The very fact of the prohibitions seemed to indicate a quality of fragility of the new democracy in Germany, a quality emphasised by the '*Spiegel* affair' in 1962. This arose out of an article in the news magazine *Der Spiegel*, which drew attention to aspects of German defence policy, and was particularly critical of Strauss, the Defence Minister. A series of Government actions, including the raiding of the magazine's offices and the arrest of members of its staff, led to bitter debates in the *Bundestag*, and the public discrediting of several members of the government, especially Adenauer himself, who seemed remarkably lacking in concern at the arbitrary actions complained of, and Strauss, who was forced to resign. Allegations of *Gestapo* methods and anti-democratic tendencies reinforced demands for Adenauer's resignation also.[3]

West Germany's relations with other states were very much the concern of Adenauer in the 1950s, once the Western Allied powers handed over control of foreign policy to the German Government in 1951. Adenauer was an early and a firm proponent of a Western alliance in which the Federal Republic would have a major role, even if this could only be achieved at the cost of setting back hopes of unification, or a

[3] See below, Chapter 7.

neutrality such as Austria achieved in 1955. In particular, Adenauer deliberately cultivated American and French links with the Federal Republic, and supported the foundation and development of the European Economic Community. These policies were accompanied by rearmament within the North Atlantic Treaty Organisation, though with a novel emphasis on a democratic citizen-army, involved in civilian society, not separated from it, and firmly under parliamentary control. The negative aspect of such policies was the growth in hostility between West Germany and the states of the Communist bloc. Diplomatic relations with the USSR were resumed (involving the homecoming of thousands of German prisoners-of-war from Russia), but the 'Hallstein Doctrine', which announced that the Federal Republic would not have formal diplomatic relations with any country recognising East Germany by diplomatic exchanges, hindered West Germany's relations with Eastern European states. In this way, the Federal Republic increased the divisions in Europe, rather than helped to bridge them.

Adenauer's political style was categorised as 'Chancellor democracy'. To a large extent, the dominant position of the Chancellor is a direct result of constitutional provision: the relatively weak powers of the President, the positive vote of no confidence requirement, the appointive powers of the Chancellor, etc., contrasting as they do with the equivalent sections of the Weimar constitution. In some ways, too, the historical situation played its part: the first years of the Republic required its George Washington to deal with the complex problems of society. But the contrasts between Adenauer and his successors, Erhard, Kiesinger and Brandt, show that personality played a large part as well. Adenauer established his supremacy in Cabinet meetings, within the party organisation (he stayed on as chairman of the CDU until 1966), and in the *Bundestag*. He extended the powers of the Chancellorship to the utmost. Electoral campaigns were designed to emphasise his personal leadership of the Government, with the party as his instrument. He was even tempted to try to be nominated for the office of President on the termination of Heuss's second period, but declined to pursue this further on discovering how difficult it would have been to stretch the presidential powers under the Basic Law. In identifying the politics of the Federal Republic so closely with his own leadership, he did the new state a grave disservice, and the task of his successor, Erhard, was made vastly more difficult.

ERHARD, KIESINGER AND THE GRAND COALITION

Erhard, an ageing 'Crown Prince', at last succeeded to the Chancellorship in October 1963 when Adenauer retired. Though there was personal animosity between him and Adenauer, Erhard continued with many of Adenauer's policies, at least in terms of general direction. The particularist foreign policy of de Gaulle made Germany's relations with France especially troublesome, despite the landmark treaty of friendship which Adenauer had negotiated, signed in January 1963. A more relaxed policy towards Eastern Europe led to trade agreements with many of the Warsaw Pact states, but relations with East Germany continued to deteriorate, and the Berlin situation (especially since the construction of the Wall separating East Berlin from West Berlin in 1961) was a source of continuing tension. Erhard did succeed in increasing the CDU vote at the 1965 election, but criticism of his qualities of decision and leadership, coupled with an obvious economic decline, led to a political and economic crisis in 1966. The victory of the Social Democrats in the North Rhine-Westphalia *Landtag* elections, the electoral gains of the extreme right-wing National Democrats (NPD) in local and *Land* elections, and the refusal of the coalition partners, the FDP, to sanction tax increases caused Erhard to lose the confidence of his party, and he was replaced as Chancellor in December 1966.

The idea proposed in 1966 of a 'Grand Coalition' composed of the CDU–CSU and the SPD was not new; it had been mooted when Adenauer set about forming his first Cabinet in 1949. The scheme had several advantages: party strife would be reduced, especially over important and sensitive issues such as foreign policy and economic strategy; the dependence of the CDU on its none-too-reliable junior partner, the FDP, would be eliminated; the SPD would acquire experience in governing at the national as well as at the provincial level, after its seventeen years of opposition; and a majority electoral system, on British lines, could be introduced in place of the proportional system, which would then probably eliminate all minor-party representation in the *Bundestag*. But such a coalition would also eliminate responsible parliamentary opposition, and would lead to increasing friction *within* parties, even perhaps encouraging extremist groups such as the NPD or the leftist groups who won for themselves the title of 'extra-parliamentary opposition' (*ausserparlamentarische Opposition* – APO).

This was the solution, however, which was devised during the autumn crisis of 1966, and following Erhard's loss of support in his own party, in the *Bundestag* and in the country, and the refusal of the FDP to form a coalition with the SPD, Kiesinger, the Minister-President of Baden-Württemberg, was elected Chancellor. He brought in Brandt, the leader of the SPD, as his deputy and Foreign Minister, while several other leading members of the SPD also received ministerial positions. Ranged against this massive ruling coalition, the only opposition was the FDP, with 49 members in the *Bundestag*.

The economic crisis was soon overcome. But in other respects the new Government faced serious difficulties. Electoral reform was proposed, a commission of inquiry appointed, but no action followed. The Emergency Laws (*Notstandgesetze*), passed in the *Bundestag* in 1968, provoked serious criticism and major protests against the Government. The surge of the NPD continued, and the left-wing opposition (especially among students) grew apace. Law and order became a major issue, overshadowing the new initiatives of Brandt in his search for 'dialogues' with Eastern European states. As the coalition partners prepared for the 1969 federal elections, their dilemma became clear. They each sought a clear party profile, but neither could denigrate the joint achievements of the coalition without, as it were, blaming themselves as much as their partners. In addition, there were signs that the public, as well as several major politicians (including Kiesinger himself), would welcome a continuation of the coalition for a further four years.

POST-WAR DEVELOPMENTS: A SUMMARY

In the twenty-two years of the Federal Republic's existence, it is equally possible to discover a case for supposing that very little has in fact altered in German political culture, or for proving that 1949 did indeed constitute a new beginning, and that the current regime is not only the first workable democracy which Germany has experienced but one of the most thoroughly democratic in Europe. As so often is the case with political generalisation, each contains much truth.

The political continuities between the Empire, the Weimar Republic, even the Third *Reich*, and the Bonn Republic are real and significant. West Germany is still a composite state, with important regional variations. Religion is still in many ways a factor in political choice. The major parties have their roots in Wilhelmian as well as post-Versailles Germany, The persistence of traditional elements in social and economic life have their influences on political procedures and political debate. The 'modernisation revolution' which commentators such as Dahrendorf have discerned is by no means complete.

Yet 1949, even more than 1945, did represent a break with the past. Secular change is evident in several areas of political life, if only because the world has changed, and West Germany is very much more involved in the world outside than it has ever been in the past. West Germany's roles in the EEC, NATO and various other international and regional bodies have forced a wider view on her politicians despite themselves. One example of this: the student protests of 1968 were a Western, not just a German, phenomenon, which German politicians had to cope with as did the politicians of France, Britain, Holland and the United States. Institutions, too, have changed. The Constitutional Court, the constitutional status of political parties, the interweaving of federal and *Land* responsibilities, the new stability of the Chancellor's position – all these have influenced German politics on their own account.

The first two decades of any new state tend to be the most crucial for its later development. In considering the Federal Republic as such a new state, it is easier to see how its past was not only relevant but different also, and how release from that past has been so important to West Germany's development as a democracy.

PART TWO

The Political System

4 The West German Political System

THE CONCEPT OF A 'POLITICAL SYSTEM'

To give analytic coherence to the complex variety of political structures and institutions in a large modern state such as the German Federal Republic, some convenient conceptual framework is required. One of the most suitable is the 'systems framework' developed by political scientists such as David Easton, Gabriel Almond and Karl Deutsch.[1] This is based on the idea that a political system can be identified analytically, by reference to the various structures and their interrelationships that are involved in the political process (which, for Easton, is the 'authoritative allocation of values', for example). Such a system is a useful model, for it emphasises the interactions among political structures, and draws attention to the key concepts of environment, feedback, stress and communication. It also facilitates relevant comparison with regimes from Germany's own past, as well as with the numerous other states of the contemporary world.

In the other chapters of this section, an account is given of the structures involved in the political process, arranged according to a simplified adaptation of the models of Easton, Almond and Deutsch. This chapter provides a brief preliminary overview of the political process in West Germany, in order to demonstrate the linkages among the major concepts (see Fig. 1).

According to this framework, inputs enter the political system from the political public, from the environment in the form of stresses of various types, and from the political authorities themselves. The political authorities convert these inputs into outputs of several kinds, such as policies or the settlement of conflict; these outputs in turn are communi-

[1] D. Easton, *A Framework for Political Analysis* (Englewood Cliffs, N.J., 1965); G. Almond and J. Coleman, *The Politics of Developing Areas* (Princeton, 1960); K. Deutsch, *The Nerves of Government* (New York, 1963).

cated as feedback to the political public, and may in their turn stimulate new inputs as a result. Political groups, such as parties and pressure-groups, have as their function the task of aggregating, amplifying, simplifying and representing the various inputs from the political public. They are, of course, themselves composed of members of the political public, and themselves often initiate inputs on behalf of their own members.

The environment of the system consists of anything outside

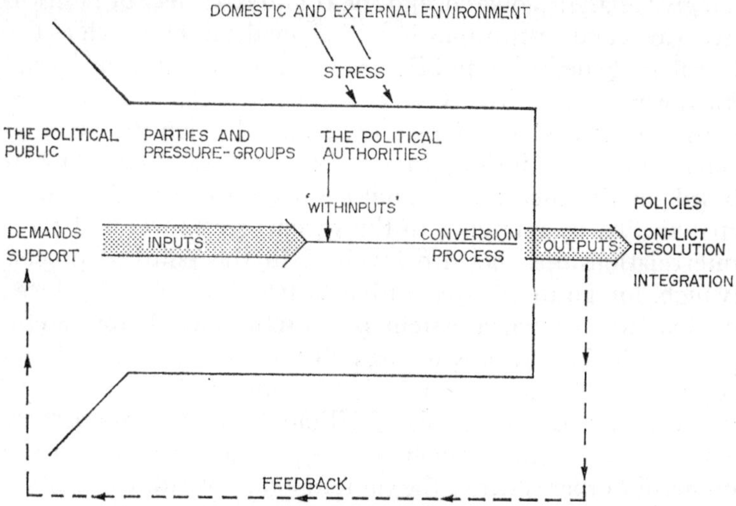

Fig. 1. *A diagram of the political system*

the system which is capable of imposing stress on the system. It is most simply categorised in two ways. There is, first, a distinction between the physical and the social environments. The Pakistani political system has recently illustrated this very clearly. The 1970 hurricane imposed stress from the physical environment; the authorities had to organise relief. In 1971 the pressures from the East Pakistan population for greater autonomy were partly an input from the political public, but were also a form of stress from the socio-cultural system, that is, from the social environment. Climate, ecology, natural resources and the distribution of the population territorially are aspects of the physical environment; social structure, economic arrangements, legal institutions are aspects of the social environment. Secondly, the environment may be classified as domestic, when it is part of the same societal system as the political subsystem, and external, arising from some other societal system or from a multi-societal system. The domestic economic system is an example of the first; the political institutions of a foreign state, or the policies of an alliance or international organisation, are examples of the second of these.

AN OUTLINE OF THE WEST GERMAN POLITICAL SYSTEM

How can these general concepts be applied to a description and analysis of the institutions, structures and processes of West German politics?

First, the three classes of political actors can be distinguished. The political public consists of those people in the Federal Republic (and, in some political contexts, West Berlin) who have the legal status, rights and responsibilities of citizens, or who, though lacking such legal status, possess political influence within the system (certain foreign residents, or adolescents below voting age, for instance). They are the source of many of the demands for policies, decisions, or other forms of 'authoritative allocations' which the political authorities must consider. They are also the source of political support. Such support may be for the authorities themselves, for the 'Government of the day'. It may be for the regime, and it is noteworthy, for instance, how much greater is the support for the current regime than was that for the Weimar Republic. It may, at a more general level, be support for the political unit itself (and there is today considerable patriotism of a West German, as well as of a German, type). The political public is also the audience for a large amount of political communication, from the authorities and from organised groups, as well as being a source of such communication itself, to the mass media, the authorities, parties and to other members of the public. But the political public, when it acts effectively, often acts in and through political groups: in West Germany through the various political parties and the assortment of pressure-groups of various types which exist. These groups perform a variety of functions in the West German political system. They filter, focus and transmit demands on behalf of members and supporters. In this way they make articulate the issues of political debate. They also themselves provide the occupants of political authority roles: the

Chancellor, the ministers in the Cabinet, members of the legislature, *Land* and local government politicians, are almost invariably party members, and frequently have interest-group affiliations also. The authorities themselves, acting within a set of rules derived from the Basic Law, legislation, custom and procedural regulations, convert the demands they receive into policies and other forms of authoritative pronouncement, as legislation or ministerial decree, for instance; they try to regulate conflicts when these are political in character; they seek to foster the integration of the political community; they respond to stresses from the environment (e.g. when German diplomats are kidnapped, or there is a recession in the economy); and they communicate with the public and with political groups concerning their policies, the state of the environment, and any other matters relevant to the political system. Such communication is the method by which information concerning the actions of the authorities is 'fed back' to the political public.

Next, various political processes can be discerned. The most obvious is the conversion of various forms of input into outputs, for instance when a law is passed by the *Bundestag* and *Bundesrat*, when a minister makes an important speech or consents to a new departmental regulation. Such inputs may have originated from the public, the parties, pressure-groups, or the authorities themselves (in which case they can be termed 'withinputs'). The system is also responsive to stresses from the environment, and the authorities can act without specific reference to the public, for instance in cases of emergency, when diplomatic pressures are brought to bear, if there is a serious alteration in the currency reserves, or if a dispute occurs in the EEC. Here again feedback takes place; these responses may elicit increased support from the public, or they may trigger a decline in support (as the talks between Brandt and Stoph, the Prime Minister of the DDR, have perhaps done). The system is also adaptive. It can change and develop in the face of pressures and stresses, by altering its operating rules, as when the Basic Law is amended, for example; by developing new structures, for instance when new departments are established; by increasing its political resources, as when the level of public spending is increased; and by alterations in its pattern, of which the proposals to change the boundaries of the *Bundesländer* is an example.

In these terms, much can be explained about Germany's past. The Second *Reich* collapsed as a result of a combination of environmental stresses and the withdrawal of support by important sections of the political public. The Weimar Republic never really developed significant levels of support, or the adaptability to survive in the face of environmental stress and increasing internal conflicts. The Third *Reich* did develop high levels of support, but collapsed as a result of an inability to cope with increasing environmental stress, stress which was a consequence of the system's own policy outputs. The strengths and weaknesses of the present political system will emerge in the following chapters, as the inputs, outputs, co-ordination processes of the political system of West Germany are considered in more detail.

5 Political Inputs

THE POLITICAL PUBLIC

Much of the business of the governmental institutions of the Federal Republic – the Cabinet, the ministries, executive agencies, and the legislatures and their committees at federal, *Land* and local level – is concerned with matters originating from the general public. As well as being the target for a wide variety of communications on political matters (see Chapter 7 below), the Government must consider carefully the demands for policies, decisions and actions made by the public. It must also ensure that the activities of the Government and the more fundamental general rules, such as the Basic Law, which regulate the procedures of the system itself, are supported by the public to a sufficient degree.

The Basic Law itself recognises this important relationship between the public and its Government. Art. 17, for instance, guarantees the right of individuals to send requests or complaints to the authorities; Art. 20 talks of authority stemming from the people through elections, voting and specific legislative, executive and judicial bodies; and Art. 21 refers to the parties' function of *Willensbildung* (taking part in the formation of the political will of the people).

Members of the public have a variety of different wants, needs, attitudes and opinions. Some of these are to do with political matters. It is only when an opinion is articulated that 'the Government ought to do something' – put through a policy, change a law, make a decision or take some particular course of action – that the term *demand* can be used. When such an opinion is voiced collectively, it is called *public opinion*. In a large and complex state such as West Germany, individual demands rarely come to the notice of the Government or the *Bundestag* except when the individual is in a highly influential position, or when the matter itself is of exceptional importance. So demands tend to be amalgamated, discussed by groups such as parties or interest-groups, and then, if enough people consider them to be of sufficient importance, they are passed on to the Government by lobbyists, put into party manifestos, given publicity by the mass media, and so thrust upon the attention of the authorities. Though, in the past, the political tradition has not been encouraging towards such pressures from the public on the authorities, whether the Imperial Chancellor or the *Führer*, it has come to be regarded as an important aspect of the democratic framework of post-war politics in West Germany that such demands should be readily and regularly transmitted.

Without minimum levels of support from the public, neither the Government itself nor, ultimately, the type of political system in any society could continue to exist. This is as true of the Federal Republic as of any other state. Such support need not always be of a positive type; negative aspects such as an absence of civil disobedience or rebellions are as important as voting or other forms of popular participation in politics. The West German authorities must thus not only decide on policies and implement them, they must ensure that such policies secure the consent of the public, and this is done in a variety of ways. First, the Government and the legislature are themselves composed of party leaders and representatives, some of whom are also spokesmen for important interests: agriculture, the trade unions, various sectors of industry, commerce, the civil service, the churches or education, for instance. So there is a large degree of presumed support implicit in the system of decision-making anyway. Secondly, interests are consulted in advance of proposals, formally and informally, and the opposition in the *Bundestag* is often informed on politically sensitive matters as a matter of course (e.g. on the substance of the 1970 Russian Treaty proposals). Thirdly, the Government takes pains to explain and defend its actions; the Federal Press Office[1] is just one of the means it has available for this purpose. The emphasis on parties and pressure-groups as intermediary institutions in the generation of support as well as the transfer of demands is clear. The way in which these groups are organised and the positions they take on major issues are central to their tasks of transmitting demands and generating support, but before

[1] See below, Chapter 7.

considering these topics, it is necessary to see how the public – again with the parties in an important intermediary position – not only influences the Government but chooses the members of the *Bundestag*, who, in turn, elect the Chancellor and thus decide which party or parties will form the Government.

THE WEST GERMAN ELECTORAL SYSTEM

The major institutionalised method for the exercising of the political influence of the public is the electoral system, which determines the composition of the *Bundestag* and affects, even if it does not actually decide, which parties will form the Government. It compels the parties to produce electoral platforms which will form the basis of the policy programmes they will present should they become the Government. It is a means by which the electorate can indicate its support of the Government, as well as its degree of satisfaction with the political system. The campaign is an occasion for a concentration of political communication of a persuasive, informative and interrogatory nature; it is an educative process for the citizen; and its symbolic as well as its instrumental functions are an important part of the political culture.

The federal electoral system in West Germany is regulated by legislation (the electoral law) under Art. 38 of the Basic Law which specifies that elections shall be universal, free, equal and secret. The electoral law has been amended several times since it was first promulgated in 1949, and today it provides for an equal mixture of directly elected constituency candidates, and candidates elected proportionally from *Land* party lists in numbers sufficient to make the total seats for each party proportional to its percentage share of the total (second) vote, once the votes for parties failing to gain representation have been deducted. The country is divided into 248 constituencies, of approximately equal size, periodically modified on the basis of reports of a Boundary Commission. In these constituencies, the electorate consists of all citizens not disqualified by the usual and specified factors such as certain types of prison sentence, and who are over the age of eighteen. Voting lists are compiled on the basis of residence as registered with the authorities; there is no special registration procedure for elections. The voter is given a ballot paper consisting of two sections. The first of these is the list of candidates for that constituency, as in Britain, with their party affiliations indicated. The candidate with the most votes on this section is elected. The second part is a schedule of the political parties which have presented lists in the *Land* in which the constituency is situated. It is on the basis of the votes for the second part that the remaining 248 seats are allocated so that, together with the members already elected directly, the total representation of each party will be in proportion to the votes it has received on the second part of the ballot paper. There is no compulsion to vote for a candidate on the first part belonging to the party for which the voter decides on the second part of the paper, and indeed in some constituencies in 1969 there were substantial differences observable. Three qualifying points need to be stressed about the electoral system. First, the proportional seats are only allotted among those parties which poll 5 per cent of the total vote in the Federal Republic as a whole (before 1953 it was 5 per cent in any one *Land*, favouring regional parties), or who have elected three members directly. This eliminates small parties, and, indeed, apart from the two major parties only the FDP have retained their representation in the *Bundestag*. Secondly, it is possible for a party to win directly more seats on the first part of the ballot paper in a *Land* than their proportional votes in that *Land* entitle them to (e.g. in a *Land* with 20 direct seats, a party could conceivably win 10 of those seats directly, yet have polled only 40 per cent of the list votes). In such a case, the party would retain its 'superproportional' representation as a bonus. Thirdly, seats are allocated from the lists not by a straight calculation of a percentage share according to its percentage vote but by the d'Hondt system of distri-

TABLE I

Results of the 1969 Federal Elections

	Votes (millions)	*Votes* (per cent)	*Direct seats*	*List seats*	*Total seats*
CDU–CSU	15·2	46·1	121	121	242
SPD	14·1	42·7	127	97	224
FDP	1·9	5·8	–	30	30
NPD	1·4	4·3	–	–	–
Other parties	0·4	1·2	–	–	–

Note: Votes are those given for the party lists, i.e. 'second votes'.

bution, by which each party's vote is divided by successive integers of the series 1, 2, 3, 4, . . ., etc., the resulting scores being placed in descending order and the seats then allocated to the highest scores. This system not only allocates the seats among the various party lists but does so in such a way that each *Land* obtains representation according to its voting turnout.

TABLE 2

D'Hondt Distribution of the First 15 Seats, 1969 Election

	Party	*Score*	*Divisor*
1.	SPD	14,065,716	1
2.	CDU	12,079,535	1
3.	SPD	7,032,858	2
4.	CDU	6,039,767	2
5.	SPD	4,688,572	3
6.	CDU	4,026,511	3
7.	SPD	3,516,429	4
8.	CSU	3,115,652	1
9.	CDU	3,019,883	4
10.	SPD	2,813,143	5
11.	CDU	2,415,907	5
12.	SPD	2,344,286	6
13.	CDU	2,013,255	6
14.	SPD	2,009,388	7
15.	FDP	1,903,422	1

Source: Wahl zum 6. Deutschen Bundestag am 28 September 1969, in *Bevölkerung und Kultur,* Reihe 8: '6. Allgemeine Wahlergebnisse nach Wahlkreisen, Sitzverteilung und Abgeordnete' (Statistisches Bundesamt, Wiesbaden, 1970). In this table the CDU and CSU are treated separately.

The electoral systems at *Land* and local level are very similar to the federal election procedures, though variations do exist, such as the one-vote system in many *Länder,* by which candidates are elected directly but which may also determine (as in North Rhine-Westphalia) the proportional distribution of seats from party lists, and the 10 per cent 'hurdle' in Bavaria rather than the 5 per cent figure used elsewhere.[2] Nor is the d'Hondt system always used for calculation of proportional distributions.

[2] In Bavaria a party must poll 10 per cent of the votes cast in one of the seven electoral districts before it participates in the proportional distribution.

Turnout in elections in West Germany is high. The federal elections of 1965 and 1969 resulted in over 86 per cent of registered electors casting their votes, and the 1970 *Landtag* elections in Hesse and Bavaria had turnouts of over 80 per cent. Voting in communal elections is almost as high. Such high turnout indicates at least formal minimum support for the system, as well as being a tribute to the intensity of party campaigning and the convenience of electoral arrangements (voting takes place on a Sunday, for instance). More dubious is the assumption that high turnouts indicate positive orientations towards the Bonn democracy, since turnout was high during the Weimar period also. Nor is it wise to assume that these high levels of turnout are also indicative of high levels of political understanding. About 5 per cent of votes are spoilt in some way, partly because some voters cast only one of their two votes. The reasons for such incomplete or invalid voting papers may, to some extent, be connected with the somewhat complicated nature of the two-vote system.[3]

THE POLITICAL PARTIES

Some of the several functions of parties in relation to the political system have already been mentioned. In terms of the inputs of demands and support, they provide an important link between the political public and the authorities. Because they have as their major purpose the winning of power through competitive elections, they are necessarily concerned with discovering what the public wants, and what policies they will most readily support, or at least tolerate. Therefore they are very concerned with identifying the opinions and attitudes of the public: the growing use of opinion polls by the party organisations is one indicator of this. The parties' platforms and programmes are designed to inform the public of the policies which the parties will press for, and are phrased in such a way as, it is hoped, to maximise the support they will attract.

Apart from election campaigns, the parties inside and outside the legislature serve as filters and amplifiers of demands, critics of Government policy (even if their party is in the Government!), and advocates of specific courses of action.

[3] R. Stiefbold, 'The Significance of Void Ballots in West German Elections', *American Political Science Review*, LIX 2 (June 1965) 391–407.

Not that the parties are entirely pragmatic: they possess their ideologies and principles, their traditional interests and the more-or-less customary sections of the electorate towards which they tend to direct their appeal. While the more general political ideas of German public life are discussed in Chapter 9 below, an overview is given here of the background, organisation, programmes and sources of support of the major parties.

The Christian Democrats (CDU) and the Christian Socialists (CSU)

These parties (which may be considered as one, since the CSU is organised only in Bavaria, and the CDU does not present candidates there) are the successors to the Catholic parties of the Second Empire and the Weimar Republic, but came to include elements of other liberal and conservative moderate parties of Weimar days, as well as absorbing in more recent years much of the following of the various right-wing splinter parties formed after the war. As politics revived in West Germany after the war, several party groups formed whose dominating theme was the 'reacknowledgement of the human and social values of Christianity'.[4] Unlike the pre-war Centre Party, these groups were multi-denominational, and two major centres of activity developed, in Berlin and in the Köln region of the Rhineland. After negotiation, conflict and, eventually, compromise among these several groups, a united party, the Christian Democratic Union, emerged in all the *Länder* except Bavaria, under the leadership of Konrad Adenauer. These fragmented origins are reflected in the higher degree of autonomy which local and regional groups possess, compared with other major parties.

Experience in the regional and bizonal administrations gave the party the opportunity to develop policies ready for the first *Bundestag* elections in 1949. Its electoral success in these and in subsequent elections, under the leadership of Adenauer and Erhard, enabled the CDU–CSU to lead governing coalitions for twenty years.

In addition to the local party organisation, the CDU has sixteen regional organisations (including one for Berlin). From these regional organisations come the delegates to the

[4] A. Heidenheimer, *Adenauer and the CDU* (The Hague, 1960) p. 32.

national party conference. Also at the federal level, there is the party presidium of eleven members, which is the effective day-to-day controlling organ of the party, though, as in the other parties, there exists a somewhat larger party executive committee with a membership of thirty, and both these bodies are elected by the conference. The chairman of the party has, so far, always been the Chancellor or ex-Chancellor, but suggestions have been made to divide this office from that of Chancellor-candidate. Within the *Bundestag*, there exist the parliamentary party organisations of the CDU and the CSU (as a *Land* group), as well as the combined *Fraktion* of the CDU–CSU for general purposes.

Financially, the party has fallen on hard times.[5] In part, this is attributable to a fall in donations after the party lost its status as governing party, in part it is due to debts from the 1969 election campaign and the costly new party headquarters being erected in Bonn. Suggestions to raise subscription dues from members have been criticised on the grounds that such a step would further reduce the already relatively low membership figure.

The Christian Democratic programme has been generally pragmatic, maintaining its Christian ethical orientation and a stance favourable to private property, business interests and social tradition, but, especially at the promptings of the influential 'social wing' of the party, ensuring that there is adequate state provision for old people, the disabled, the unemployed and other disadvantaged sections of the community. Its social-market economic policies were typical of this mixture of welfare and libertarian orientations. In foreign policy the CDU has sought to strengthen West Germany's ties with the West, especially through NATO and the EEC, but there has been a readiness to negotiate with the Communist states of the East when this has seemed advantageous. Itself a broad coalition of interests, the policies of the party have had to accommodate the several varied elements of its voting support; its ability to remain in the Government until 1969 is a mark of the success of this. Its main support has come from regular church-attenders, especially Catholics; women voters; the older voters; farmers, salaried employees and the self-employed: regionally it has been strongest in North Rhine-West-

[5] *Der Spiegel*, 29 Mar. 1971, p. 44: 'Ein Bettelorden'.

phalia, Schleswig-Holstein, Bavaria and the south-western *Länder* of Saarland, Baden-Württemberg and Rhineland-Pfalz.

The Social Democratic Party (SPD)

Unlike the CDU, which was formed as such only after the Second World War, the SPD has a history reaching back to the uniting of two workers' parties at Gotha in 1875. Despite Bismarck's repressive socialist legislation, the party flourished, and under Weimar was generally the largest of the many parties. Banned by the Nazis, it re-emerged as strong as ever after the war. Organisationally, it has always been an extremely centralised party, based on a relatively large subscribing membership (whose dues provide a large proportion of its income) organised into local and regional groupings. At the national level there exists the *Fraktion* (parliamentary party organisation), a small but powerful presidium of ten members (which, unlike the CDU and FDP, is elected by the executive rather than the party conference), a larger executive, and a national conference which normally meets every two years, and which is formally the highest authoritative organ of the party.[6] The conference elects the executive. The chairman of the party has usually, but not always, been the party's candidate for the Chancellorship (e.g. Schumacher, Ollenhauer and Brandt). In 1968 the position of general secretary was created (*Bundesgeschäftsführer*) whose broad responsibilities are concerned with the organisation and planning of electoral campaigns for the party (which, at federal, *Land* or communal level, occur every year) and with the oversight of the party organisation.

The party was in opposition for the whole of the period between 1949 and the formation of the Grand Coalition (though it provided many *Länder* Governments during that period) and only began to approach the CDU share of the federal vote after the important Godesberg Congress in 1959. This congress, after considerable inner-party debate, accepted a new basic programme for the party, far less ideological than before, and which symbolised the non-Marxist and more widespread appeal which the party sought to make. Its policies still contrast strongly with those of the CDU in some

[6] Section 17 of the Organisation Statute of the SPD, 1968.

fields, on economic affairs, democratisation of the workplace, a greater emphasis on social security even at the expense of higher taxation and heavier charges on industry, and in the new *Ostpolitik* (East European policy) which has attempted to improve relations between the Federal Republic and Russia, East Germany, Yugoslavia, Poland and other countries to the east.

The party's main support still comes from the wage-earners, especially those in trade unions (though there is not the close and formal political connection between party and unions that exists in Britain). Professional people have recently voted SPD in increasing numbers. It enjoys a majority among male voters, young voters and voters in large towns. Non-denominational and Protestant voters support it more than do Catholics. Regionally it is strongest in Hesse and the city-states of Bremen and Hamburg. Its main internal problem is pressure from the Young Socialists (*Jusos*) to increase the emphasis and priorities given to socialist policies, even when the consequence would appear to be a loss of electoral support and perhaps an end to the SPD-led coalition.[7]

The Free Democratic Party (FDP)

Formed in 1948 as a union of an assortment of Liberal and Democratic parties, which were themselves the successors of the Weimar liberal parties, the Free Democrats have been an eclectic but often divided organisation, based on non-socialist reform in certain areas of public life, but with a free-enterprise and individualistic orientation. Organisationally it has never been a strong party, and the regional-level organisations have been more powerful than the national leadership, in part because of differences of policy and attitude in the different *Länder*. It has been a coalition partner now to both the CDU and SPD at both federal and *Land* level, but since 1969 seems to have settled for a left-wing policy at the expense of losing its more nationalist and old-fashioned Liberal voters. This has resulted in unencouraging performances in recent years. The party only just achieved the necessary 5 per cent at the federal election in 1969, while in the *Land* elections in 1970–1 it lost its representation in the Saarland, Lower Saxony and Schleswig-Holstein parliaments, though its

[7] *Der Spiegel*, 1 Mar. 1971, pp. 21–9: 'Sozusagen die Macht'.

performances in Hesse and Bavaria were more encouraging. Its new leader, Walter Scheel, is determined to revive the party as a reformist organisation, but its disappearance after the 1973 elections is not unlikely.

Minor parties

Several minor parties still retain hopes of influencing national politics by their existence outside, if not inside, the *Bundestag*. Of these, the National Democratic Party (NPD) has come nearest to being represented in the *Bundestag*, when it polled just under 5 per cent in the 1969 federal election. It had a series of *Landtag* election successes from 1966 onwards, but in 1970–1 lost its representation in all the *Land* parliaments in which it held seats, such as Hesse and Bavaria. Its extreme right-wing policies are not new; they have been pressed in similar form by a series of minor parties since 1945,[8] but they found a temporary response as a result of the economic troubles of 1966 and the more skilfully organised administration of the NPD, compared with its predecessors. The revised version of the Communist Party (DKP) in 1969 supported an *ad hoc* electoral party, the Action for the Democratic Progress (ADF), but it only gained about one-half of 1 per cent of the total national vote, after a colourful and very unorthodox campaign. In the *Landtag* elections of 1970–1 the DKP presented candidates in its own name, but with little success in terms of votes. Faced with the anti-Communist attitudes of many voters in West Germany, as a result of the intransigence of the East German Communist Government, for instance, it seems highly improbable that the Communist Party will ever be of more than marginal electoral significance, especially during the lifetime of a socialist-led coalition. Of the other parties, the Europe Party polled about 50,000 votes in 1969, but lacked any clear impact in terms of personality or policy; the Bavarian Party polled about the same number (in Bavaria only, of course), but their only effect electorally may be to encourage the particularism and the right-wing stance of Strauss and the CSU. The All-German Party (GPD) gathered 45,000 votes, mainly in Hesse, Lower Saxony and Bavaria – three of the *Länder* with borders with

[8] K. Tauber, *Beyond Eagle and Swastika: German Nationalism since 1945* (Middletown, Conn., 1967) *passim*.

the East German state. Three other parties presented themselves in 1969, with minimal success. From time to time, no doubt, new parties will appear, be defeated and be forgotten. The newly formed National Liberal Action (NLA), consisting mainly of renegade Free Democrats, is the latest of these. Even with the retention of a proportional system of voting, West Germany seems to be moving inexorably towards a two-party legislative politics.

When the Grand Coalition was formed, the opportunity arose to amend the electoral law by agreement between the CDU–CSU and the SPD, in order to introduce a British-style majority system, or some variant of it. This would have produced a two-party *Bundestag*, the trend towards which has been obvious since 1949. A commission was set up in February 1967 by the Minister of the Interior, and reported in 1968 in favour of single-member constituencies and majority voting, but, partly because of fears within the SPD that such a system would operate disadvantageously to their party, no legislation was introduced. Despite the near-miss of the NPD in 1969, it seems clear that, should the FDP fail in 1973 to win the necessary 5 per cent of the total vote, the two-party *Bundestag* will be a reality, and, what is more, a permanent reality, since it is less and less possible for small parties to secure sufficient support to get over the 5 per cent hurdle, owing to increasing campaign costs, the problems of national organisation and the difficulty of finding policy positions not pre-empted by the major parties.

TABLE 3

Towards a Two-Party Bundestag

	1949	*1953*	*1957*	*1961*	*1965*	*1969*
	(percentage share of the vote)					
CDU–CSU and SPD	60	74	82	82	87	89
Other parties	40	26	18	18	13	11

Again in reaction to Weimar experiences, and as a protection against the rise of either a neo-Nazi or left-wing anti-democratic party, the framers of the Basic Law inserted provisions that political parties should be democratic in their own internal organisation, should be publicly accountable for their funds, and should not be hostile to either the existence of the Federal Republic or the democratic order which is its system of government.[9] These provisions gave the Government the opportunity to secure the prohibition of the Socialist Reich Party (SRP) in 1952, and the Communist Party (KPD) in 1956.

More positively, West German parties are the only parties in a major democratic state whose organisation and internal procedures are regulated, at least in outline, by a party law (the *Parteigesetz* of 1967). This sets out minimum provisions concerning, e.g., the programme, internal elections, meetings of the national party conference, arbitration procedures within the party and party finance. Under this law, and as a result of subsequent decisions of the Constitutional Court, parties receive subsidies from public funds equivalent to 2.50 DM per vote received at the last federal election, if they polled a minimum of one-half of 1 per cent of the total vote.[10] However, parties must publish an audited annual statement of their income in the official gazette (*Bundesanzeiger*), including specific listing of any donation, whether from an individual or a group or organisation (such as a business firm), if it exceeds 20,000 DM.

TABLE 4

Party Income, 1968

	CDU	*CSU*	*SPD*	*FDP*
Total income (millions DM)	34·4	10·1	48·0	10·0
of which:				
Membership dues	6·9	1·3	18·9	1·2
Other dues (e.g. from members of the *Bundestag*)	2·9	0·9	3·8	0·7
Donations	5·1	2·0	2·5	2·1
Public subsidy	17·7	5·3	19·7	4·5
Other income	1·8	0·6	3·1	1·5

Source: *Bundesanzeiger*, 21 Oct. 1969.

[9] Art. 21 of the Basic Law.

[10] A Constitutional Court decision in December 1968 reduced the previous qualifying figure of 2½ per cent.

PRESSURE-GROUPS

Political parties are not the only groups in West German politics which transmit the demands and support of the public to the political authorities. A variety of other groupings – lobbies, interest-groups, associations – that can be collectively referred to as pressure-groups also represent the wishes of sections of the public to the authorities, try to gather support for their demands, and, in doing so, contribute to the political processes of the Federal Republic. Such groups differ from parties primarily by virtue of the limited nature of their interests, and the fact that they wish to *influence* the Government, rather than *become* the Government, and they vary far more than do the parties in their size, organisational form, aims, resources, supporters and, most important of all, in the intensity of their political activity. Some groups are engaged in the political process almost daily, others only on very infrequent occasions. Some groups are permanent, others are *ad hoc* organisations for the achievement of limited purposes. Finally, groups differ also with regard to the type of aims which they have – economic, political or social – and it is on the basis of this division that a brief survey of some examples of the more important and influential groups can conveniently be undertaken.

Economic groups

Three major categories of economic pressure-groups can be identified: the trade unions, the employers and the agricultural interest. Of course, on many occasions, unions and employers will be in combination: when a particular region or industry is threatened in some way by a Government decision, for instance. But in general, the interests of employers and employees will be distinct, and on many issues they will look to the Government for favourable action or decisions, or, if such actions and decisions already taken appear to threaten their interests, they will seek to prevent them passing into law, or at least to modify their implementation. As in Britain and the United States, both employers and employees are organised in groups at various levels, local, regional and national, and both have national federated organisations which speak and act collectively for several national groups of a more specialised nature. For the employers, the major organisation is the Federation of German Industry (*Bundesverband der deutschen Industrie*) which represents a high proportion of firms, especially the larger ones, in West Germany, and has a record of successful intervention with the Government on several issues, such as cartel legislation and worker participation in decision-making (*Mitbestimmung*). For the employees, the German Federation of Trade Unions (*Deutscher Gewerkschaftsbund*) represents sixteen large unions to which some 6½ million members (about 30 per cent of all employees) belong. Both these organisations engage heavily in political activity, and both are regularly consulted by the Government on legislation relevant to their interests. In addition, both have contacts among the many businessmen, wage-earners and union officials who are themselves members of the *Bundestag*.[11] The agrarian interest – sometimes called the 'Green Front' – is represented by several bodies, the chief of which is the German Farmers' Association (*Deutscher Bauerverband*). The traditional view that a strong agricultural sector is important for Germany, the concentrated voting power of farmers in certain rural constituencies, and the substantial bloc of farmers with seats in the *Bundestag* all work in favour of the protection of farming interests.[12]

Political groups: the refugees

The refugees and expellees have been an important minority group in West German politics since the end of the war. By 1950, one-fifth of the population of West Germany were refugees, and in 1967 the proportion was still 15 per cent, reaching 25 per cent in Lower Saxony and Schleswig-Holstein. The main political demands of the refugees have been to be allowed to return to their homelands in the east (a matter, in part, for West German foreign policy) and, until then, to be protected from discrimination and economic hardship in their 'temporary' localities in the Federal Republic. This has been met in part by the 'Equalisation of Burdens' legislation passed in 1952. The refugees have sought to exercise political

[11] In the 1969 *Bundestag*, 265 of the 518 members (including Berlin deputies) were trade union members (*Der Spiegel*, 25 May 1970, p. 65: 'Wort Entzogen').

[12] On agricultural policy, see below, Chapter 11.

influence through pressure-groups (based in the main on cultural associations for each 'lost territory' such as Danzig, Silesia or the Sudetenland) at *Land* and federal level. Some of this influence has been channelled through a special Ministry for Refugee Affairs (abolished in the Brandt reorganisation of departments in 1969, its responsibilities being included in the Ministry of the Interior). Refugee political parties have been formed, but the local concentration of voters and the peculiarities of *Land* and federal electoral systems have restricted their success. Within the other parties, except for the NPD and, to a lesser extent, the CSU, the refugees have not managed to establish themselves as in any way a crucial element deserving of special attention electorally. Their general right-wing attitude in foreign affairs has proved somewhat embarrassing, especially to Brandt's *Ostpolitik*, where the refugees have been influential in a protest group called *Aktion Widerstand* (Resistance Action) that was founded in Würzburg in 1970. However, the continuing integration of refugees into the political community, the unreality of expectations concerning any significant changes in the Communist states' attitudes to their return, and the economic advantages of residing in West Germany have all weakened the political influence of the refugee groups even among their own members.

Social groups: (i) *the churches*

The political influence of the churches, particularly the Catholic and Evangelical denominations, is still strong, especially on matters of conscience, social welfare, educational policy and certain aspects of foreign policy. The system of church taxes (by which taxpayers in the Federal Republic have a sum deducted for the denomination of their choice, though they can 'contract out') not only gives the churches considerable financial resources but also enables them to claim to speak for a nominal following much larger than the church-attending element of their supporters. In the past, during election campaigns, the Catholic church in particular has not hesitated to advise its followers, by letters from bishops, sermons and personal exhortations, to vote only for parties which uphold the Christian faith and for candidates of Christian principle – which is often assumed to exclude the

SPD.[13] Though the frequency and effect of such interference is now declining, a controversial case still occurred during the North Rhine-Westphalia *Landtag* election in 1970, when five Catholic bishops issued a letter calling on the faithful to vote only for candidates who represent Christian principles.[14] The churches also have political influence through several ancillary organisations, which can act with less inhibition than the church itself as lobbyists when legislation is in prospect in which the churches might have an interest. The activities of the churches as agents of political socialisation, directly and through their confessional schools, are also considerable.

Social groups: (ii) *the student movement*

A movement is far less highly organised than a pressure-group; it is also less specific in its goals, and may contain several separate organisational structures within it. Its leadership also tends to be diverse. Student activity in politics since 1967 has been as a movement in these terms. It has been broadly left-wing, with reformist and revolutionary sections, and several different and often competing groups of a variety of degrees of organisation. Its main concerns have been with university reform; opposition to anything that its leaders denounce as anti-democratic or extreme right-wing, such as the emergency laws, the NPD, Strauss or the Springer publishing firm; anti-Americanism, especially expressed through opposition to the Vietnam war; the promotion of collectivist policies such as co-determination in industry (*Mitbestimmung*); and a generally favourable stance towards contacts with Communist states, including *de jure* recognition of the German Democratic Republic. Though often a highly visible, publicised and disruptive element in German politics, especially in large cities such as Munich and Berlin, the student movement in terms of politics (as contrasted to life-style) can mobilise only small proportions of the student population. Other students take part in politics through the established party organisations and their youth movements, while many others are not interested in the rather ineffectual round of

[13] U. Kitzinger, *German Electoral Politics* (London, 1960) chap. xi.
[14] *Der Spiegel*, 8 June 1970, p. 49: 'Hilfe der Hirten'.

protests, 'sit-ins', demonstrations and leaflet production that characterises student politics. Nevertheless, there is reason to think that the Government has been more aware of student opinion as a result of the growth of the student movement, and the sensitivity of the students to possible encroachments on democracy is some guarantee for the preservation of democratic politics in West Germany.

Social groups: (iii) *the Army*

In view of its past activities in German politics – its influence on the policies of the Second Empire, its powers during the First World War, its ambivalent attitude to the Government in the Weimar period, its political roles in the Third *Reich* – the Army cannot be omitted from any overview of the major groups with potential influence on the politics of the Federal Republic. In the years following the surrender of Hitler's armies several ex-officers were involved in revived right-wing activism, and when Adenauer committed West Germany to rearmament within the Western Alliance there was considerable opposition from ex-soldiers to the idea of becoming 'mercenary troops' for the Western powers in their quarrels with Russia. But once it was decided that a new Army should be formed, the greatest care was taken that it should not be independent of the civil power, nor foster attitudes of authoritarianism associated with the Prussian militarism of the past, and also that its members should, through a process of internal reform and education, have every opportunity of acquiring positive orientations towards democracy as 'citizens in uniform'. Despite fears of the reliability of the higher officers in some possible future period of internal stress,[15] and indicators that garrison troops provided higher-than-average

[15] 'Under the circumstances, one may well wonder how German military leaders would react to the breakup of the CDU and the creation, on its Right, of a nationalist conservative party or to the forming of a Socialist government. Would they exercise strictest constitutional self-restraint if a future government were to acknowledge publicly the permanent existence of two separate German states, bring about a *détente* with Russia, and renounce all claims to the territories east of the Oder–Neisse line? In short, where would the military stand under conditions of severest internal tension?' (Tauber, *Beyond Eagle and Swastika*, p. 315). It is interesting to note how many of these hypothetical events have now taken place (1971) without so far giving rise to the slightest rumour of overt military intervention in the political process.

support for the NPD,[16] there has been no reason to assume that such policies have been unsuccessful. In West Germany, as in the United States and Britain, the Army has assumed its place as a servant of the regime, rather than its arbiter.[17]

The strategies open to pressure-groups are affected by the political culture of the Federal Republic, its institutional structure, and the nature of the issue under consideration. In general, pressure-groups may seek to influence members of the *Bundestag* directly (and indeed may have supporters or officials among the ranks of the legislators), but party discipline on issues of importance is usually strong enough to neutralise any counter-pressure from interest-groups. They may try to influence parties in order to have favourable planks included in party platforms at election time, or persuade the *Fraktion* as a whole to support their case in the *Bundestag*. They may seek to mobilise public opinion in various ways. A group may threaten to advise its supporters to change their party allegiance at the next opportunity. Efforts may be made to influence departments for purposes of affecting legislation originating from those departments (e.g. farming policies, transport legislation) or to make the implementation of such legislation more favourable where departmental discretion exists. Added to these, there are institutionalised opportunities from time to time through the work of departmental advisory committees, pre-legislative consultation, and commissions of inquiry, where the opinions of affected or interested groups may be represented formally.[18]

CONCLUSION

This survey of the linkages provided by parties and pressure-groups in West Germany has pointed to their importance in aggregating, amplifying and transmitting the demands of in-

[16] R. Wildenmann and H. Schatz, 'Das Wahlverhalten an Bundeswehr-Standorten', in R. Wildenmann (ed.), *Sozialwissenschaftliches Jahrbuch für Politik*, vol. I (Munich, 1969) pp. 61–153.

[17] For further discussion of the post-war armed forces in German politics, see below, Chapter 11.

[18] 'In view of the complicated nature of modern legislation it is understandable that nowadays the bureaucracy in the ministries has become the main point of contact for organised interests' (W. Hofmann, 'The Public Interest Pressure Group: The Case of the Deutsche Städtetag', *Public Administration*, XLV 3 (autumn 1967) 257).

dividual citizens, in representing sections of the community, and in generating support for the post-war democratic regime and the various Governments within that regime. Indeed, the activity and the level of membership of parties and pressure-groups is itself in some ways an indicator of the viability of democratic politics in West Germany. That the continued efficiency of such political groups also depends on effective communication, with their membership, the general public and the authorities, will be further considered in Chapter 7.

6 Political Outputs

THE CONVERSION OF INPUTS

The inputs discussed in the last chapter – especially demands and support – are converted by the political authorities into outputs. These authorities are, at the federal level, the two chambers of Parliament (the *Bundestag* and the *Bundesrat*), the Chancellor, his Government and the civil service, and the President. They are linked to the political groups and the public in several ways: through the electoral system, through their overlapping membership of parties and interest-groups, and through constitutional rules which constrain their powers and define responsibilities in relation to the community.

The outputs of the authorities consist of legislation, administrative decisions and actions, and communications of various kinds, in response to stresses from the environment, demands from the public, parties and pressure-groups, or the needs of the authorities themselves (withinputs). Such processing is not automatic; many demands are ignored or rejected by the authorities, even when pressed on their attention by powerful groups (indeed, simultaneous demands may be mutually contradictory). Nor is such processing simple; the transformation of demands into policies, or the promotion of public support, are costly activities, owing to constraints on resources such as time, political skills, money and political power. Support is also an important factor, and many of the outputs of the authorities, especially those 'withinputs' originating from the Government, are intended to increase support so that the Government can continue in office (e.g. 'electioneering' budgets, favourable legislation for key minorities) or to generate the political resources it requires for the production of controversial and costly policies.

THE AUTHORITIES

Parliament

The West German Parliament consists of two chambers: the *Bundestag*, directly elected by a mixture of simple-majority constituency and proportional-list systems, and the *Bundesrat*, consisting of delegates of the *Länder* Governments, representation varying with the population size of the *Länder*,[1] who vote as a *Land* bloc. Parliament has many of the usual functions of parliaments elsewhere: legislation, control of the executive, control of taxation and expenditure, and the debating of political issues, as well as two which are less usual: the selection of the Chancellor, and control of the military.

Both houses are organised and controlled on the basis of party representation. This, plus the fact that the Chancellor and his ministers are, almost invariably, leading members of the coalition parties and have seats in Parliament, gives the *Bundestag* in particular an important linking role in the political system. It is here that important issues are discussed, formally and openly; it is here that the Government can be called to defend its actions and, if necessary, face the sanction of a constructive vote of no confidence, which, if successful, will replace it with another Government; it is here that the opposition parties can put their case and demonstrate their suitability for office to the public.

The work of the *Bundestag* is organised under the supervision of an all-party Council of Elders, which includes among its responsibilities the selection of committee chairmen, and the securing of party agreement on the scheduling of business. The President of the *Bundestag*, a leading member of the largest party,[2] and equivalent in many ways to the British or American Speaker of the House, is elected by a secret ballot of the members at the first meeting of a new *Bundestag* or when there is otherwise a vacancy, and, besides

[1] *Länder* have a minimum of three votes (Saarland, Hamburg and Bremen) and a maximum of five (North Rhine-Westphalia, Bavaria, Baden-Württemberg and Lower Saxony). The others have four votes each.

[2] But not, therefore, necessarily of the governing party or parties. Kai-Uwe von Hassall (CDU) was re-elected by a large majority by the *Bundestag* elected in September 1969, but there was some controversy concerning whether the largest party was the CDU–CSU (which the SPD regarded as *two* parties, and indeed for some purposes in the *Bundestag* they are treated as two) or the SPD.

presiding over plenary sessions, has responsibility for the domestic arrangements of the *Bundestag*. Many of the norms and formal rules of the *Bundestag* have been inherited from the past, but changes in the type of regime and in the institutional structure of the *Bundestag* itself have necessitated the development of new rules and practices.

The central task of Parliament is legislation. This may be introduced, as with the majority of measures, by the Government, or by the *Bundesrat* or a minimum of fifteen members of the *Bundestag* (see Fig. 2). Government bills are first sent

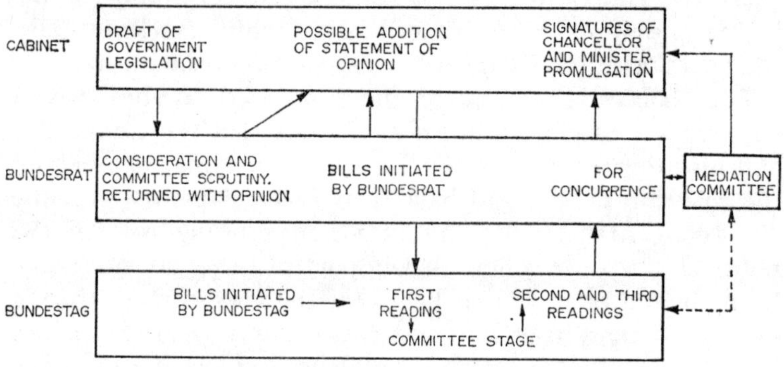

Fig. 2. *The process of legislation at federal level*

to the *Bundesrat* for consideration, though not for approval or rejection. Otherwise all bills start their legislative obstacle-race in the *Bundestag*. There a first reading is taken on the general principles of the bill. If approved at that stage, the bill is sent to one (or several) of the *Bundestag* committees for detailed consideration, at which stage representatives of affected interests, members of Government departments and representatives of the *Bundesrat* may be heard. This is followed by second and third readings, during which the bill is given more thorough consideration than at the first reading, in terms of its details, and amendments may be submitted (though the procedure for treaties is rather different in this respect). From the *Bundestag* bills go to the *Bundesrat* for their approval. The *Bundesrat* has an absolute veto on bills directly affecting the *Länder* (e.g. by the alteration of certain types of taxation, or a requirement of administrative action by the *Länder*), and a suspensive veto on other matters. The suspensive veto can be overridden by a simple majority in the

Bundestag (or, if passed by a two-thirds majority in the *Bundesrat*, by a two-thirds majority in the *Bundestag*). A conference committee of members of the two houses may be convened in order to settle differences on a bill. Legislation which has gone through all these stages becomes law after the signatures of the Chancellor and the responsible minister have been received, and when the President has also signed the bill.

The function of control of the Government is mainly the work of the opposition parties. This is exercised through debate on legislation, and through control over the budget (see below, p. 80), but more particularly through the question hour with which each plenary session of the *Bundestag* commences. This follows British practice, with notice being given to ministers (though this notice can be as short as two hours if the President admits a question as 'urgent'), and supplementaries at the discretion of the President. The *Spiegel* affair was first raised in the *Bundestag* through questions.[3] Question hour has tended to replace the more cumbersome device of interpellation, a more formal procedure by which a minister's actions may become the subject of a debate. The constructive vote of no confidence is the ultimate sanction for the opposition, for by this means it can replace the Government, but only by securing a majority for a Chancellor-candidate of its own.

Members of the *Bundestag* spend much of their time on committee work, either as members of the seventeen standing committees,[4] or in the *Fraktion* working-groups which are divided on the basis of subject-areas such as economic policy and foreign affairs. Membership of *Bundestag* committees is allocated by the d'Hondt system,[5] in proportion to party strength in the *Bundestag*. Unlike the United States system, the chairmanships of *Bundestag* committees are allocated not solely on a seniority basis, though seniority may be important, and the opposition has a share of chairmanships. Sessions of these committees are secret, and the committees may call on ministers, civil servants, specialists, interest-group represen-

[3] See below, Chapter 7.

[4] These committees are listed in Appendix A below. There is provision in the Basic Law (Art. 44) for the creation of committees of investigation, but these have been set up only infrequently.

[5] See above, Chapter 5.

tatives or anyone else to provide them with information. It is the standing committee that plays a key role in shaping the details of legislation, and it is in such committee sessions that the enthusiastic back-bencher can establish a reputation for ability and expertise, though specialisation is obstructed to some extent by the fact that most deputies must be members of at least two committees. The *Fraktion* working-groups are designed to allow members of each party interested in particular topics to discuss what the party's attitude to pending legislation should be, and what tactics should be adopted in supporting or opposing it.

It is not easy to generalise about the role of the *Bundestag* member. Some are ambitious and active; others regard their function as being that of a passive supporter of the party line. Some see membership of the *Bundestag* as a route to higher political office; others view it as a supplementary occupation to their extra-parliamentary career. However, once elected, every deputy finds himself in an occupation which is poorly rewarded financially, compared to the higher positions of the civil service or responsible work in industry, for example. The political independence of the deputy is at once subordinated to the discipline of the *Fraktion* leadership and to the pressures of his constituency (if he has one) and local party organisations. His main contribution to the work of the *Bundestag* will be in its standing committees, though again assignments to these are determined by the *Fraktion*. He will probably not speak often in the plenary session of the *Bundestag* (about 20 per cent of the members account for two-thirds of the speeches). He will be the target for the importunities of lobbyists, interest-groups and local organisations, and the recipient of constituents' complaints. He is provided with the usual legal immunities (Arts. 46 and 47 of the Basic Law), but despite the recently opened high-rise *Bundestag* building, office accommodation will probably be inadequate, secretarial and research facilities severely limited. The working conditions and career prospects of the member of the *Bundestag* thus attract professional men, especially lawyers, civil servants (whose tenure is safeguarded through their legislative careers), journalists, and professional officers of party, trade union and other interest-group organisations – that is, people who can combine two careers with success, and where membership of the *Bundestag* may be an advantage in terms of the extra-parliamentary occupation. The possibility that leading *Land* politicians will enter the Cabinet without being members of the *Bundestag* at the time (perhaps even becoming Chancellor, as Kiesinger did) limits the opportunities for advancement for back-benchers. However, this works in reverse. *Bundestag* members can find high positions in *Land* Governments, as Kuhn, the present Minister-President of North Rhine-Westphalia, has done. Köppler, his opponent from the CDU in the 1970 *Landtag* elections, also left Bonn to seek fame in Düsseldorf.

Though this section on Parliament has concentrated on the *Bundestag* – a concentration also reflected in the mass media in West Germany – the *Bundesrat* also has significance in any consideration of the outputs of the West German political system. It has a role in the policy process (outlined above), and in the production of support, on a *Land* basis, for the system. The modern *Bundesrat* is the successor of the federal second chambers of the imperial and Weimar regimes, and was designed by the framers of the Basic Law as a representative chamber of the *Länder*, and thus also as a counter to the centralisation processes which occurred in the last years of Weimar and in the Hitler period. Its powers *vis-à-vis* the Federal Government and the *Bundestag* derive from the constitutional requirements that it be consulted on legislation initiated by the Government, and that it must approve legislation affecting the *Länder* and concur in other legislation. However, it is neither a mere reflection of party strengths in the *Bundestag* or the country – and fears that the CDU would use its majority there after 1969 in order to block the SPD–FDP coalition's legislation have proved unwarranted – nor of party attitudes. Rather it is a 'bureaucratic' chamber, concerned with the protection of *Land* interests and, to a large extent, with the administrative aspects of legislation which the *Länder* will have to implement if it passes into law. This orientation is in part due to the predominant role of *Land* civil servants in its committees (only *Land* ministers attend the plenary sessions), but this bureaucratic concern may be regarded as a valuable counterweight to the more politically oriented proposals of the Federal Government and the *Bundestag*. Despite the potential for friction which exists by the very nature of the *Bundesrat* – in Parliament, but not of it – the care taken by departments in drafting Government legislation so that problems with the *Bundesrat* do not arise, and the work of the conference committee of the two chambers, which is nearly always able to find suitable compromises, has meant that surprisingly little conflict between the *Bundesrat* and either the Government or the *Bundestag* actually occurs. One expert has commented that 'the *Bundesrat* is in a unique position to bridge the gap which twentieth-century critics believe to exist between accredited policy-makers and those who actually make policy by administration'.[6]

The Chancellor and his ministers

During the long term of Adenauer's Chancellorship, the phrase 'Chancellor democracy' was used to describe his superior powers in relation to the *Bundestag*, his Cabinet colleagues and his party. The successors of Adenauer have not been able to present the same easy superiority, or have not wished to, and the Chancellor today, though still the most important member of the political system, is much more reliant on his colleagues and his party than was Adenauer.

The Chancellor is nominally selected by the *Bundestag*, but nominated by the President. In practice, the electorate and the political parties do the choosing, for it is most unlikely that anyone other than the leader of one of the two major parties would find a majority in the *Bundestag*, except in some abnormal circumstances. The President, therefore, has the task after an election of discovering which leader has succeeded in forming a coalition able to command a majority in the *Bundestag*, and then nominating that person. The *Bundestag* must then vote without debate, and a simple majority of the total membership suffices to elect.[7] Only in 1969 was there any doubt as to which of the two major parties would provide the Chancellor, and in this case the decision of the FDP to support Brandt was decisive. In the event of a constructive vote of no confidence being passed by the *Bundes-*

[6] E. Pinney, 'Latent and Manifest Bureaucracy in the West German Parliament: The Case of the Bundesrat', *Midwest Journal of Political Science*, VI 2 (May 1962) 164.

[7] If a candidate cannot be found who commands such an absolute majority, a majority of those present and voting may suffice at a later stage (Art. 63 of the Basic Law).

tag, the procedure requires that a majority be obtained for a new Chancellor, so here again the discretion of the President and of the *Bundestag* would be limited to acceptance or rejection of the nominee of the challenging party. The Chancellor, after election, then selects his ministers, and they are appointed by the President.

The political role of the Chancellor is determined partly by the Basic Law, partly by the precedents set by his predecessors, and partly by the combination of his own personality and the context of the contemporary political situation. The Basic Law (Art. 65) provides that the Chancellor shall determine general policy guidelines for the Government, and be responsible for such policy. Indeed, since formally his ministers are not responsible to Parliament, he must accept such formal responsibility and face dismissal by the *Bundestag* if necessary. The Chancellor is able to control his ministers by demanding to be notified of their plans, by receiving reports, by his chairmanship of Cabinet meetings and by the ultimate sanction of dismissal. He also has the power to rearrange departmental responsibilities and reduce or increase the number of departments and Cabinet posts. Though the dominant position of the Chancellor which gave rise to the phrase 'Chancellor democracy' to describe West Germany's political style has not survived Adenauer's term as Chancellor,[8] the precedents set by Adenauer have at least meant that Erhard, Kiesinger and Brandt have enjoyed a primacy in the Governments they have led which, but for Adenauer's earlier assertions of authority and policy initiative, might have been more closely questioned. The chairmanship of his party and his acceptability to the coalition parties other than his own will also be important factors. Adenauer and Erhard both suffered from loss of confidence by their own party, the CDU, and by their FDP junior partners, towards the end of their terms, which weakened their political effectiveness. It could well be that in future a compromise Chancellor may emerge, whose political backing enables him to play only a co-ordinating role as chairman of the Cabinet, rather than a strong initiating role.

[8] Professor Ridley has written that Chancellor democracy 'may simply be another description for the Adenauer Era' (F. Ridley, 'Chancellor Government as a Political System and the German Constitution', *Parliamentary Affairs*, XIX 4 (June 1966) 460).

Ministers are selected by the Chancellor, usually from among the leading members of the coalition parties. Bargaining over the distribution of posts in a coalition may take as long as bargaining over its policy programme. Though under the broad direction of the Chancellor on policy matters, ministers are given the responsibility under the Basic Law for the control of their departments (Art. 65). Ministers are members of the Cabinet, but important State Secretaries may also attend Cabinet meetings, though they are members of the civil service. The departments are organised on a functional basis for the most part.[9] The chief posts, after the Chancellor, are those of Foreign Minister, Economics Minister and, at least under Brandt, the Minister for Special Tasks responsible for the Chancellor's Office. The ministries of the Interior, Defence, Finance and Justice are also important. Other ministries tend to be less 'political' and more 'technical' in their interests, though they may well be involved in political controversy, especially with their relevant interest-groups: Agriculture; Transport, Posts and Telecommunications; Education and Science; Labour; Housing and Health are in this category. Though the *Bundestag* has no formal powers to dismiss ministers other than the Chancellor, it can censure them, question them, and make its dissatisfaction known in a debate. Should a minister become a political liability, he would probably be dismissed by the Chancellor. Strauss (following the *Spiegel* affair) and Oberländer (a Minister for All-German Affairs with a dubious background relating to the Third *Reich*) were both forced to leave Adenauer's Cabinets by external pressures.

More recently a kind of junior ministerial post has been created, first in a few departments, now in all of them: the Parliamentary Secretary of State. These were introduced in the period of the Grand Coalition, and extended by Brandt. These members of the *Bundestag* deputise for their ministers in the legislature and the Cabinet, and may be made responsible by the minister for a special area of the work of the department, or some particular project.[10]

[9] For a list of current ministers, see Appendix B below.
[10] R. Zundel, 'Gehilfe oder Ober-Minister?', *Die Zeit*, 19 Dec. 1969.

The civil service

It would certainly be unrealistic, in considering the outputs of Governments of modern political systems, to neglect the role of the civil service. The West German civil servant, recruited usually by his department, belongs to one of four grades, corresponding to the educational standards required for entry. The highest grade (*der höhere Dienst*) is filled almost exclusively by graduates with law degrees, a training which, as Dahrendorf has noted,[11] colours attitudes towards political matters. The post-war civil service still retains many of the characteristics of the pre-war civil service, particularly with its emphasis on status and security, and its bureaucratic efficiency. However, the increasing complexity of government, with regard to the technical and the political tasks with which it must be concerned, has necessarily thrown more responsibility than ever on the higher levels of the civil service, as well as demanding of them new skills and new attitudes. It often happens that the State Secretary (the chief civil servant in a department) is better informed about the matters with which his department must deal than is his minister, who may be newly appointed to Cabinet office, or recently transferred from a different department. In any case, ministers have the broad tasks of supervising policy, and parliamentary duties and party responsibilities as well; the specifics they must delegate to their administrators. Thus the external contacts, committee work, relative permanence and ability to concentrate on relatively narrow areas of policy which civil servants possess give them influence on the drafting of legislation, the opportunity to affect its details in sessions of *Bundestag* committees, and responsibility for its implementation. Nor are they unaware of the demands of the public, or at least of certain sections of the public, for many of them have regular contact with interest-group leaders, *Länder* and community Governments, the mass media and other sources of opinion. Of course, much of their discretionary power depends on their relationship with their ministers, but in many cases this is a close and trusting partnership rather than a superior–subordinate relationship.

[11] Dahrendorf, *Society and Democracy in Germany*, pp. 240–1.

The President

The framers of the Bonn constitution deliberately made the office of Chancellor more powerful than it had been under the Weimar regime, at the expense of presidential powers. The President still has important rights and duties, but politically these are very restricted and conditional. There have been three Presidents since 1949: Heuss, Lübke and Heinemann, elected by a special Federal Convention, consisting of the members of the *Bundestag* and an equal number of members elected by *Land* parliaments, on the basis of proportional representation. The term of office is five years, with a two-term limit. A leading West German political commentator, Theodor Eschenburg, has distinguished five functions of importance which the President has been given by the Basic Law.[12] First, as head of state, he represents the Federal Republic to other states. It is he who signs treaties, accredits ambassadors and receives foreign diplomats. Secondly, he has certain powers of control over, e.g., the appointment of the Chancellor, and possibly other ministers, and in cases of legislative emergency. He has, thirdly, a right to be consulted on certain promotions and appointments of higher civil servants, judges and other officers of state, and will expect the Chancellor to consult with him on any matters of a politically sensitive or crisis nature. Fourthly, he is an arbitrator when a Chancellor is elected in the *Bundestag* on the third ballot with only a relative majority, for he can accept such a nomination, or dissolve the *Bundestag*. Finally, he is, like most heads of state, a conciliator in the event of a political crisis of any kind. The danger is always that the official eminence of the office might tempt a President to greater political interference than the Basic Law envisages. Adenauer, aware of such possibilities, did indicate in 1959 that he might resign from the Chancellorship to seek the President's office, but later advice told him how limited politically the office would be.[13] So far, the powers of the office have in any case been little tested.

[12] 'Was darf der Präsident?', *Die Zeit*, 7 Mar. 1969.
[13] Heidenheimer, *Adenauer and the CDU*, pp. 222–9.

THE POLICY-MAKING PROCESS

Policy outputs from the West German political system may, as described above, be the result of parliamentary legislation. Other policies may be the product of administrative action, where new legislation is not required for some reason. Whatever the process in any particular case might be, it is clear that policy-making in West Germany is the consequence of the interactions of a complex set of political structures, usually involving at some stage interest-groups, political parties, Parliament, the Government, some of the federal departments and quite possibly *Land* and community authorities as well.

To simplify the investigation of this complexity, it is useful to conceive of policy-making as a sequence of seven stages. These are: *initiation*, when a policy proposal is first put 'on the agenda' of the policy-making authority; *information*, the process of gathering data about the policy alternatives available, their costs and advantages, the problems of implementation, etc.; *consideration*, which consists of assessment of the various available courses of action (including perhaps those of not having a policy at all, or postponing further progress); *decision*, the act of choosing one of the alternatives which have been considered; *implementation*, the means by which the policy decision is converted into action; *evaluation* of the policy's effects in relation to its aims; and *termination or re-initiation* as a result of such evaluation. Of course, depending on the type of policy and the particular policy-making institutions involved, some of these stages may be telescoped or even occur simultaneously (information and consideration, for instance), and the sequence might contain 'loops', i.e. certain previous stages might recur before progress is made to a further stage (consideration back to information before going on to decision, say).

In the case of policies of the Federal Government of West Germany, the initiation stage occurs when a minister brings forward a policy proposal for the Cabinet agenda, or, if the matter is not of such importance, when he starts to plan a particular policy within his department. Such proposals do not simply originate from nowhere. As has been seen in the previous chapter, they may be the result of demands from the public, either direct and immediate, or via the programme of the governing party which the voters have accepted at the last election. A policy may be a response to environmental stresses, such as a disaster, an economic crisis or the actions of a foreign power. It may be a 'withinput' – an idea from the minister himself or one of his civil servants which is considered deserving of attention and action. Information may be gathered in various ways, by committees of inquiry, by departmental research, by data collection by an external organisation under contract (a public opinion polling firm, for instance) or from the advisers to whom the ministry looks for relevant intelligence, such as the council of the heads of the five major economic institutes who meet together to prepare reports on the West German economic situation. In some cases, either there will be little need of new information, or no time available for its collection. But since policy-making implies rational procedures (if not necessarily rational behaviour), to ignore the gathering and presentation of information altogether would be to reduce the policy process to a lottery. For the consideration stage, the Cabinet or other relevant institution marries the available information with its priorities and the specific aims which it intends to achieve through the policy in question, and takes into account the alternative courses of action open to it.

Here an interjection is necessary. For policies requiring legislation, at this stage the parliamentary process is interposed (see above, p. 68). Indeed, a separate cycle of policy-making is commenced in Parliament, with initiation, information and consideration as the various stages of debate, and committee discussion, in the *Bundestag*. The votes on the proposal are the decision stage, but usually these are predetermined by party discipline, thus demonstrating the difference between the formal and the 'real' policy-making process.

Otherwise, if legislation is not required, the Cabinet or the minister will make the decision by selecting the particular policy to be implemented, or deciding not to have a substantive policy at all, or going back to a previous stage of the process. In either case – legislative or administrative decision – implementation will be through the civil service or the administrative structures of the *Länder* or local authorities, or other agencies such as the courts, the diplomatic service, the military or economic undertakings in which the state has a responsible role. Evaluation may occur later, but remarkably few policies are ever formally evaluated by the policy-making authorities, except where some definite time limit is built into the life of the policy, or where something goes very wrong. The policy may then be terminated, by repeal of legislation, for instance, or a different policy may be initiated, or the decision may be made simply to continue with the current policy.

In all the stages of the policy-making process, the work of the new planning staff in the Chancellor's Department has considerable potential significance. Originally created in 1967 as an aid to the Chancellor in his general task of 'determining policy guidelines', under Brandt the size of the staff has increased rapidly, its functions have become more extensive and ambitious, and it is a crucial component of the 'new-style' governmental structure which Brandt and Ehmke have sought to introduce in order to co-ordinate more effectively the disparate plans and policies of the departments. The planning staff, aided by experts from external organisations such as university institutions, have the tasks of providing plans and data for long-term policies of the Government; the co-ordination of short-term projects, in terms of Cabinet priorities, financial considerations and similar factors; the investigation and improvement of planning and information procedures in the Federal Government;[14] and the investigation of basic questions of structural reform in the Government, such as the greater use of Cabinet committees. The planning staff relate with departments through departmental planning commissioners (who usually rank just below the State Secretaries, so are influential within their departmental hierarchies), and also have frequent meetings with *Land* administrators and with the staff of specific departments, to improve co-ordination and exchange ideas and experiences. In an attempt to improve the co-ordination of the future plans of the Government, a data-processing system has been introduced, by which the departments regularly provide the Chancellor's Department planners with standardised information concerning the progress and probable consequences of their projects – in terms, for instance, of the effects on the economy and the likely political importance of the

[14] 'Brandt soll mit KIS und Orakel regieren', *Die Welt*, 3 Dec. 1970.

project.[15] The proposals contained in the Government Declaration have been listed as a set of detailed projects, and long-term planning horizons have been introduced: for finance until 1974, education until 1980, and transport until 1995, for example. Many obstacles have been encountered which have restricted the progress of this ambitious planning concept: departmental autonomy, especially on the part of large and important departments which have been planning their own policies for a long time past; concern at the power such a planning staff confers on the Chancellor, and his Minister (Ehmke) as well; a lack of suitable staff and tested methods for undertaking such ambitious planning exercises; and, ultimately, the tendency of the Cabinet to ignore recommendations of the planners in their concern with immediate political pressures. But if the general concept of more rational planning becomes more widely accepted within the Government, the contributions it can make through the provision of information, the development of more reliable methods of comparing alternative policies and their consequences, and the evaluation of ongoing policies, will all be of immense assistance to the Government in its task of matching outputs to the demands of the public and the imperatives of an increasingly complex social system.

Another co-ordinating mechanism is the budget. This is presented to the *Bundestag* by the Minister of Finance, as a comprehensive bill of planned expenditures and revenues. While other members of either chamber of the legislature may propose increases in Government expenditure, these require the Government's consent, which leaves financial control firmly with the Cabinet. However, parliamentary scrutiny is strict, and budget debates are generally lively and controversial. In terms of policy-making, since few policies of the Federal Government can be implemented without imposing additional costs, the budget is an important check on policy priorities. The appropriations committee of the *Bundestag* plays a strategic role in the budgetary process, partly because of its own expertise, partly because of shortage of time available to the *Bundestag* itself.[16]

[15] 'Der Macher', *Der Spiegel*, 1 Feb. 1971, pp. 32–4.

[16] G. Loewenberg, *Parliament in the German Political System* (Ithaca, N.Y., 1967) pp. 374–5.

SOURCES OF POLICY

This picture of policy-making in the Federal Republic would not be complete without a look at the sources of policy. The policy-making process itself has been assumed here to begin with the initiation stage, when an item is put on an agenda for consideration. But why are certain policies pursued, and not others? What determines priorities? What are the values which lead a Government to choose one of the policy alternatives available in preference to another?

In Chapter 5 it was shown how the demands of the political public reached the authorities generally through the intermediary agencies of political groups. Since the Government and the two legislative chambers are composed of politicians who are party members, and, in many cases, who possess group affiliations or sympathies, it is not surprising that the first answer to the questions posed above is that priorities and values are related to a large extent to these party and interest-group affiliations. For example, the fiscal policies of the Brandt Government with regard to, say, reform of the income tax are based directly on the section on 'Healthy Finances: The Basis of Socio-political Reforms' in the 1969 electoral programme of the SPD ratified at an extraordinary party convention on 17 April 1969 in Bad Godesberg. But in turn this section of the electoral programme itself derives from the more general passages in the section on 'Income and Property Distribution' in the Basic Programme of November 1959, ratified also at Bad Godesberg. The Godesberg Programme itself was an articulation of the basic political values of the party membership at the time. Of course, other considerations affect the outcome of such policy. The 1969 Government was formed as a coalition, and the junior party, the FDP, has some expectations that it will be able to modify major policies in line with its own party programme 'Practical Policies for Germany: The Concept of the FDP', which it drew up at the twentieth party congress at Nürnberg in June 1969. The economic and political context must also be taken into account. Too much attention and too many resources devoted to aspects of taxation reforms, for example, could leave insufficient time, energies or political resources for, say, educational reform or foreign policy. A mistimed proposal might be overtaken by an economic depression, or a change in the international economic situation, and so on. A good guide to current and prospective policy proposals is the Government Declaration made by the Chancellor at the beginning of each term of office.

Not all policies derive from the needs of an articulate public, filtered by parties who may assume governmental office, nor from the ideas and ideals of the parties themselves. A pressure-group, perhaps representing only a small minority, may also influence the direction and shape of a particular policy. It may do this by proposing a change in some policy, as did the veterans of the *Waffen-SS* when they were excluded from the pension distributions made to other ex-soldiers, or trade unionists pressing for *Mitbestimmung* (employees' participation in managerial decisions) as a policy for industrial undertakings. Or it may be defensive, seeking to block policy proposals, or at least amend them drastically: peace groups opposed to rearmament in the 1950s; industrial groups blocking cartel legislation in the period 1952–7;[17] wine growers incensed by unfavourable aspects of the EEC proposals for wine in 1970; refugee groups opposed to Brandt's policy of *rapprochement* with Russia and the recognition of the Oder–Neisse border between Poland and Germany in 1970. The *Länder* also have their demands. These are often channelled through the *Bundesrat* or negotiated with ministries, but, though sometimes of considerable importance, seldom receive very much publicity.

Yet another source of policy, and, in terms of the amount of Government attention perhaps the most important, is the Government itself. It has the fundamental responsibilities of preserving and protecting the state, responding to crises, and generally managing the day-to-day affairs of the nation. Circumstances frequently do not permit the consultation of an affected interest-group, an election manifesto or a special convention of party delegates before action is taken. The kidnapping of a West German diplomat, a disaster in Pakistan, the need to stimulate the economy or respond to pressures

[17] G. Braunthal, 'The Struggle for Cartel Legislation', in J. Christoph and B. Brown (eds), *Cases in Comparative Politics* (Boston, 2nd ed., 1969).

from the East German Government, the latest trade figures, student riots in a major city – these require swift reactions from the Government, the production of a policy which may not be the best possible if time were available for longer consideration, but which copes at least adequately.

Whatever the source of policy, it requires support for its implementation, and alongside the planning of the policy itself the Government must ensure that its aims and intentions are properly explained to those affected. Here the Federal Press and Information Office has an important role,[18] as have the mass media in their reports and commentaries, the speeches of the ministers, and the constituency work of members of the *Bundestag*. Finally, the policies 'feed back' to the public. Their effects may stimulate new demands, and the input–output process starts all over again.

POLICIES AND POLITICAL SUPPORT

This chapter, like its predecessor, has concentrated on the political system at the national level, but it must be remembered that many of the important areas of policy-making competence – education, town planning, crime prevention, public health, the administration of justice – occur at the *Land* level. Though the *Land* policy-making process is little different from that at the national level, and parties and pressure-groups play similar roles to those they take nationally, the scale may be very different, as may the types of policies. There are wide differences in the scope and the subjects of policy-making between Bavaria and the Saar, or between the city-state and port of Hamburg and the agrarian *Land* of Schleswig-Holstein.

At *Land* and at federal levels, the elected political authorities are more than mechanisms for converting pressures for policies from the public into statutes, decisions and governmental actions. They are also the objects of support for the political public, legitimated by election according to processes laid down in the Basic Law and by implementing legislation. They may not please most of the people most of the time, but they can count on a considerable degree of acceptance for their decisions and actions by virtue of their election by the

[18] See below, Chapter 7.

public, supplemented by their explanations, in public and in private settings, of why such policies were necessary. This support depends very much on the existence of effective channels of political communication and feedback in the political system.

7 Political Communication

COMMUNICATION AND FEEDBACK

The operations of a political system, by which the demands of the political public are converted into policies and actions by the political authorities, depend on effective communication procedures, and on the existence of feedback mechanisms which provide the authorities with information about the effects of their outputs. Indeed, the very survival of the system, as well as its adaptation to stress and its possibilities of development, are related to the quality of communication which the authorities receive about the current state of the system, the system's past (its 'memory'), and its environment.[1]

The German Federal Republic and its predecessor regimes afford particularly trenchant examples of the important role played by political communication in the political system. The Ems telegram was a key factor in the events leading to the unification of Germany. The chaos and revolutions in Germany in 1918 were intensified by poor communication to the people of the true state of the military situation on the Western Front, so that Germany's sudden surrender came as a great shock, and permitted the 'stab in the back' legend to flourish later. The perceptive propaganda policies of Hitler and Goebbels helped to discredit Weimar and establish the dictatorship which followed it. The military collapse in 1945 was worsened by the failure of Hitler to obtain (or want to obtain) a true assessment of the situation on the Eastern Front. De-Nazification and 'education for democracy' were carried out in all four zones by the occupation authorities (though with different aims in view) by the careful use of the mass media, and the licensing of newspapers in the Western zones.[2] Since 1949, political communication has been of importance as an instrument of policy, an integral part of elec-

[1] K. Deutsch, *The Nerves of Government* (New York, 1963) p. 129.

[2] L. Clay, *Decision in Germany* (London and New York, 1950) chap. 15.

tion campaigning, an area of political controversy and a feedback mechanism by which Governments at all levels, federal, provincial and local, can be made aware of sectional and general opinion on a wide range of matters.

THE MEDIA OF POLITICAL COMMUNICATION

Broadly, the media of political communication in West Germany are similar to those of other Western industrial societies. When examined in more detail, however, certain specific differences of importance become apparent. In part, the framework of political communication is regulated by the Basic Law.[3] It is also affected by the way in which political communication in the past has been intertwined with political events.

The media of personal communication are those to be found also in Britain, the United States and France, for example. Modern industrialised societies depend on, and develop, high levels of interpersonal communication, and when the political system has democratic form, such communication is a requirement for its continuance and development. The formation of opinions; discussion of political matters; the right to demand, protest, oppose; the freedom to communicate personally with members of the legislature or the Government; all these are subsumed under the term 'democracy' and all presuppose a high level of interpersonal communication. In West Germany such communication can make use of comprehensive postal and telephone networks, run by the state, and a set of opportunities for face-to-face communication which include, in political contexts, open political meetings organised by the political parties and various interest-groups; closed meetings for members of those groups; the *Stammtisch* at the local pub; interviews with members of the local council, the *Land* parliament or the *Bundestag*; and a growing habit of private conversation about politics which no longer has to fear the spying of neighbours or the reports of the blockwarden. Though in the recent past there has been some concern about 'wire-tapping'[4] and the

[3] For example, Art. 5 (relating to freedom of expression, censorship, etc.) and Art. 10 (secrecy of the mails).

[4] See, for instance, *Der Spiegel*, 11 Jan. 1971, pp. 31–3: 'Die Staatsräson ist kein vorrangiger Wert'.

secrecy of the mails, in general the private and personal media of political communication are available as a means of free expression of political opinions, the articulation of political demands, and the transmission of political information. However, the reluctance of the older generation of West Germans, especially, to become personally involved in politics or political controversy has meant that these personal media are not used as intensively for political communication as they are in, say, Britain or the United States, where the local MP and Congressman is more readily regarded as a source of information or assistance, where political campaigning in the form of doorstep or telephone canvassing is more traditionally established, and where the custom of political discussion in small groups has been able to continue unimpeded by totalitarianism or occupation by a foreign power. Here again an interesting feature of West German politics must be explained in terms of institutional, historical and cultural factors. However, in recent elections (such as those observed by the author in 1969 – the federal campaign – and 1970 – the North Rhine-Westphalia *Land* elections) the parties have begun to place greater emphasis than before on stimulating the involvement of the voter, by doorstep and street-corner canvassing (though not for purposes of discovering and recording party sympathies, as in Britain, but rather to persuade and inform, and to make the party and its candidate known to the voters, and by replacing speeches at party meetings with question-and-answer sessions. In part, this has been a result of left-wing and student pressure for 'democratisation' of the electoral process; in part, it is a consequence of the involvement of young people in politics, as voters, supporters and candidates; in part, it is a result of doubts about the ability of mass-communication methods to inform the voter adequately about candidates, specific party proposals or general political orientations, and has been used especially by the two parties who have recently laid stress upon their more modern and altered 'images' – the SPD and the FDP.

Political communication, though, is more usually associated with the mass media: television and radio, newspapers and magazines, posters and pamphlets, all of which carry undifferentiated messages to large numbers of people relatively swiftly and cheaply.

Radio and television broadcasting in the Federal Republic is based on *Länder* or multi-*Land* regions, and controlled by public corporations on which a broad range of interests and social groups are represented: the trade unions, the churches, education, etc. The second television channel was started in 1963, in competition with the first channel, which commenced transmissions in 1952. A third, mainly cultural, channel was introduced in the *Länder* at various dates in the late 1960s. Ownership of radio and television receivers is widespread. At the end of 1968 there were nearly 19 million radios licensed in the Federal Republic (including West Berlin), which is equivalent to about one for every three inhabitants. In addition, there were almost 15 million television sets licensed, or one for every four inhabitants. Programmes of political relevance include news broadcasts, news commentary and magazine programmes, a variety of discussion programmes (such as the popular Sunday morning programme, *Internationale Frühschoppen,* consisting of discussion by foreign journalists of political themes) and transmissions of important debates (e.g. on the budget or the Russian Treaty) direct from the *Bundestag*. At election time there are many more broadcasts, including the usual (though strictly rationed) crop of party 'commercials', and comprehensive coverage of the results.

Though fears have been expressed that party representation on the controlling bodies of radio and television may be both disadvantageous to the quality of programmes and a means of improper political regulation of programme content,[5] these have not been justified to any great extent by events so far. The parties grumble, as they do in Britain, about unfair presentation of their views,[6] and it is true to say that so far no real crisis has occurred to tempt the parties into political management of the broadcasting media, but in general the standard of impartiality of West German radio

[1] See, for example, K. Sontheimer, 'Hochgejubelte Studenten?', *Die Zeit,* 8 Nov. 1968.

[6] A study by the WIKAS research institute on time allocation in news programmes in July 1970 showed a bias of about 4:1 in favour of the governing coalition over the opposition, in terms of time, and twenty-five politicians were shown from the coalition, against only fifteen of the CDU–CSU. This was, however, probably a function of the importance of the role of the Government rather than party bias, and the month chosen was not very typical ('Barzel war nicht im Bild', *Die Zeit,* 11 Dec. 1970).

and television seems as high as anywhere in Europe.

The Press, in contrast to broadcasting, is in private ownership, though the dominant position of Axel Springer (owning around 40 per cent of daily newspapers in terms of circulation, in West Germany and West Berlin) is still very much a matter of political concern. The Allied powers' licensing policy helped to establish a varied and non-Nazi-influenced range of publications after the war, and in 1949, when licensing came to an end, the West German Press was one of the major pillars of the new democratic political system. Few newspapers are tied to a political party, though most have an identifiable political orientation. The choice of Bonn as the federal capital (where no major daily newspaper is published), and the fragmentation of production of the major newspapers among several cities such as Hamburg, Frankfurt, Stuttgart and Munich, has meant that West Germany has no national daily newspaper, even though several, such as the *Frankfurter Allgemeine Zeitung*, *Die Welt*, the *Stuttgarter Zeitung* and the *Süddeutsche Zeitung*, achieve national circulation. But in the first quarter of 1969 there were over 500 daily papers, selling only some 21 million copies in total (in Britain, by comparison, the *Daily Mirror* sells nearly 5 million copies, the *Daily Express* around 3 million copies).[7] Such statistics starkly reveal the parlous economic state of the West German newspaper publishing industry, and its necessarily local emphasis. The Government Declaration of Brandt in October 1969 stressed the concern of the new coalition over the condition of the West German Press, and promised legislation.

Politically, the newspapers cover a wide range of views, and the separation of news and commentary is fairly clear in most papers. As in Britain, the conservative orientation is more widely represented (especially in the Springer papers) than among the electorate as a whole, but this is counterbalanced to some extent by the weekly magazines, many of which have an anti-establishment orientation. Among these *Der Spiegel* is an especially renowned organ of criticism of Governments, politicians, big business and various other institutions of West German society.

[7] *Bild Zeitung* sells about 4 million copies daily, *Die Welt* less than a quarter of a million.

Political communication, except at election times, or in terms of basic orientations and political socialisation, is generally confined to the media mentioned above. Poster advertising is used extensively in election campaigns, as also are pamphlets of various kinds. The Government uses posters and pamphlets to inform the public of certain policies, or as part of a campaign of persuasion (e.g. on road safety, or the operation of a census). Books, the cinema and the theatre are other, less common, forms of political communication, but generally of political attitudes and opinions than of specific information, except for school or college texts. The lessons of the Nazi past, with its multifarious propaganda channels, and the censorship and indoctrination policies of Communist states, inhibit the overt employment of 'cultural' media for political purposes. None the less, there is a growing tradition of political cabaret in some cities such as Düsseldorf, Munich and Berlin, and the works of, for example, Grass, Hochhuth, Böll, Brecht and Enzensberger must not be excluded from a survey of political communication in contemporary West Germany, especially in view of the political controversy their works still arouse.

Because of the past, and because of the emphasis placed by the re-education and reconstruction policies of the occupation powers on the mass media as crucial elements in the establishment of a democratic regime in the Western zones of Germany, there has been a particular sensitivity in West Germany to signs of political interference or control over the mass media. Three major examples of this sensitive concern have been the *Spiegel* affair of 1962, the controversy over the second television channel in 1961, and the problem of the Springer publishing firm.

The Spiegel affair

'Even had there been no Third *Reich*, the *Spiegel* affair would have raised significant questions about the state of health of the West German political system.'[8] As it was, only a dozen years after the founding of the Bonn Republic, the events which occurred aroused extreme concern about the depth of democratic attitudes, at least those possessed by leading politicians. Following publication of an article on West

[8] R. Bunn, *German Politics and the Spiegel Affair* (Baton Rouge, La, 1968) p. xvii.

German defence policies, the *Spiegel* offices in Bonn and Hamburg were raided on 26 October 1962 by officers of the Government, and files were removed for investigation. The editor, Rudolf Augstein, and several of his staff were arrested (one while on vacation in Spain). On learning of these actions, the FDP members of the coalition threatened to resign, and a storm of accusations and counter-accusations were made in the *Bundestag*, during which Strauss, the Minister of Defence, admitted personal responsibility. During the interchanges, Strauss evaded certain questions, and apparently misrepresented facts on others, and, despite Adenauer's defence of his minister, Strauss resigned his post as Minister of Defence. Several remarkable features emerged from the affair. One was that, balancing the reluctance, to say the least, of the CDU–CSU leadership to place freedom of the Press before their own opinions and interests, the protests of the FDP, SPD and several extra-parliamentary groups against the actions of the Government were encouraging indeed for the continuation of democratic politics in West Germany. On the other hand, Strauss returned to a ministerial position in 1966, unweakened, it seemed, by the accusations which had been levelled against him. *Der Spiegel* has continued more successfully than ever as an organ of radicalism and criticism. But there are no grounds for confidence, as yet, that such an affair could not recur, given a conjunction of circumstances involving an authoritarian Chancellor, and the somewhat ambiguous roles of the legal system and the civil service still unchanged.

The second television channel

Perhaps inspired by his knowledge of the close association between de Gaulle's Government and the television service in France at the time, Adenauer attempted in 1960 to set up a second television channel in West Germany, under Federal Government control. This would have been an alternative to what he perceived as an over-critical first channel. A bill was prepared to carry this proposal into effect, but considerable opposition was aroused, and in 1961 a case was brought before the Federal Constitutional Court. The Court ruled that broadcasting was a *Land*, rather than a federal, responsibility, and Adenauer somewhat grudgingly accepted this ruling.

The *Länder* proceeded to set up their own joint second channel based on Mainz (ZDF – *Zweite deutsche Fernsehen*), with a controlling body on which all the *Länder* are represented. Once again, the issue showed the sensitivity that existed concerning Government control of the mass media, especially in the light of memories of Hitler's broadcasting monopoly in the Third *Reich*.

The Springer empire

The growth of the Axel Springer publishing empire has led to increasing concern about Press ownership because of its rapid expansion to a position of dominance in the newspaper industry. In some cities its share of newspaper circulation approaches 90 per cent. Its popular tabloid, *Bild Zeitung*, may be regarded, for all its unsubtle sensationalism, as politically the most influential single journal in West Germany. The right-wing and nationalist political views of the Springer papers, coupled with the excuse of Press concentration and the more specific reason of attacks by Springer's papers on left-wing and student demonstrators, led in 1968 to students in Berlin attacking the Springer headquarters there, and attempting to prevent lorries delivering newspapers from leaving the building.[9] In May 1967 a commission was set up by the Government to investigate concentration of ownership of mass media, with Springer himself as a member. Its report did not include any very practical recommendations for restructuring the newspaper industry, though since its report Springer has divested himself of some of his holdings in certain publications to other owners. The Government Declaration made by Brandt in October 1969 promised that legislation on Press concentration would be forthcoming.

THE FUNCTIONS OF POLITICAL COMMUNICATION

Several functions of political communication in the political system of West Germany can be distinguished, with regard to the public and to the authorities. The main functions are those of the transmission of information, political persuasion, political learning and political integration.

It is important that the Government should be able to obtain information about society (both in the past and in the

[9] *Der Spiegel*, 22 Apr. 1968, pp. 48–50.

present), about the effects of its own activities (feedback), and about the environment. There is an almost unlimited range of possible sources from which such information can be obtained. The mass media are available to inform the Government, as well as the public. The Government controls its own information sources: records, reports of inspectors, advisers, overseas representatives, its information office, the statistical office with its headquarters in Wiesbaden and so on. It will receive communications from members of the *Bundestag*, from the parties, from organisations, from members of the public. It can commission investigations and surveys, set up committees of inquiry and arrange for the collection of new forms of data. These information sources are similar to those in other Western democracies, but it is noteworthy that in West Germany there is perhaps a greater awareness of the need for a Government to be kept well informed of the reactions of the public, and that there is a duty to do so, especially in view of the rigidly controlled channels of political communication in West Germany's neighbours to the east, and the propaganda record of the Third *Reich*.

The Government Press and Information Office is a particularly interesting institution in relation to political communication from and to the Government. This office was set up in 1949 within the Chancellor's Department, and is independent of other departments (which also possess their own Press sections). The Director of the Office answers directly to the Chancellor. He does not have Cabinet rank, though he regularly attends Cabinet meetings. The Office has the tasks of providing information, culled from domestic and foreign sources, such as newspapers, broadcasts and reports of various kinds, to members of the Government, and in turn informing the public at home and abroad, often via the news media, of the achievements and policies of the Federal Government. Its staff of some 650 carry out these functions in a variety of ways: by means of Press conferences, special publications, briefings, public opinion surveys, the distribution of digests of news to departments of the administration and monitoring of broadcasts, for example.

Because of its wide range of functions, touching all the various departmental interests within the Government, and because, in a sense, 'information is power', the status and control of this Office has been, and indeed remains, a sensitive political question. The temptations, for example, to blur the distinction between publicising the work of the Government, and the achievements of the parties which compose that Government, are very real, especially at election time.[10]

One especially important source of information for the Government is the opinion poll. Surveys are carried out regularly by several of the main polling organisations such as EMNID (Bielefeld) and the Allensbach Institute, dealing with the degree of support for the Government and for leading political personalities, attitudes towards particular policies, and more general orientations towards, e.g., the Bonn regime, the Hitler period and democracy, for instance.

Political information can also be obtained by the public in many ways. Except among the minority with a relatively high degree of interest in politics, such information will usually not be sought; it must be presented in such a way that it is readily available to its audience. Usually it is only at election time that there exists any great readiness to give attention to political messages beyond the television news programmes or the newspaper lead stories.

This also makes the task of political persuasion more difficult, as is shown particularly at elections. The campaign managers have little specific information to guide their selection of media, their slogans or their levels of expenditure beyond custom, 'what the others are doing' and the results of opinion surveys. To some extent, their publicity strategies are constrained by law, or by party agreement, e.g. over the division of the scheduled party broadcasts on television, or the period and amount of poster advertising. Beyond that, the aims seem to be (*a*) to create voter awareness of the fact that an election campaign is under way, and (*b*) to persuade them to vote for a particular party or candidate. To achieve these aims, a mix of Press advertising, television and radio party broadcasts, posters, leaflets, loudspeakers and cinema vans, meetings and parades is used to achieve a 'scattershot' effect, on the assumption that if the voter misses one item of publicity, he'll hardly miss them all.

Such persuasive campaigning is becoming increasingly professional to the extent that outside consultants are used. In

[10] See, for example, Kitzinger, *German Electoral Politics*, pp. 108, 263.

1969, for instance, the FDP used the TEAM agency at Düsseldorf, the SPD used the ARE advertising firm, and the CDU called on the services of three agencies. These firms integrate the publicity efforts of the party which employs them, and attempt to improve the efficiency of the campaign in terms of scheduling and expenditures. Surveys are used to obtain subtle information for the parties (e.g. the SPD choice of orange as the 1969 campaign colour was a result of surveys which showed it to be regarded as a 'young, dynamic, active' colour), as well as more straightforward data about voter preferences and attitudes. Between one-third and one-half of central campaign expenditure in 1969 was devoted to Press publicity, while far less reliance was placed on television party broadcasts than is the case in the United States or Britain.

As it has become more professional, persuasive communication has also become more centralised. In the 1969 federal election campaign, even at the constituency level, there was little attempt to emphasise local or *Land* issues, despite the fact that, in several of the *Länder*, elections for *Land* parliaments would be occurring in the following twelve months, and despite the existence of several local issues which could have been exploited. Like the media, however, the message was also standardised. Many candidates used a common format for election addresses, for instance, in which a photograph of the candidate and a short personal message were inserted into a standard centrally produced statement of party policy. In *Land* elections the same trend is noticeable, reinforced by the knowledge that the outcomes of such elections are increasingly important nationally, both in determining the composition of the *Bundesrat* and in deciding the fate of the SPD–FDP coalition.

The demands of the public on the political authorities also involve persuasive communication. Pressure-groups seek to persuade the Government directly, through the political parties, and through the electorate, of the merits – or at least of the force – of their case. During election campaigns, such groups may issue leaflets, insert advertisements in newspapers, draw attention to their case at political meetings and in other ways attempt to influence the election of candidates or parties favourable to their aims. When the Government announces its intention of pursuing a particular policy, as with the rearmament issue of 1951–3, the Emergency Laws of 1968 or the *Ostpolitik* of 1970, groups write to the newspapers and to members of the *Bundestag*, meetings and demonstrations are arranged, posters appear, speeches are made in Parliament and in a multitude of ways sections of the public seek, by communicating their opposition, to alter the actions of the Government.

Informative and persuasive communication have as an important by-product political learning. The Government learns from its mistakes (and its successes), as the effects of its policies are communicated by feedback channels. The SPD–FDP coalition, for instance, is learning that a Government led by Social Democrats does not necessarily find it easier to obtain a moderation of wage demands from the unions; the Christian Union parties, in opposition, may learn that the tasks and opportunities of an alternative Government are of a different quality from those of a Government that had been in office for two decades. In both cases the cohesion and efficacy of the parties in their changed roles depend to a large measure on their ability to preserve open communication channels within the party organisations (hence the appearance at the 1970 Young Socialists' conference in Bremen of Brandt, Schmidt and Wehner, for instance) and between the party and the public. The policy-planning staff of the Chancellor's Department may also, by improving the communication process in the civil service, provide the previously somewhat isolated ministerial departments with the opportunity to learn from each other's experiences.

The public also learns through political communication. This is a major element of political socialisation,[11] the process by which people acquire their norms and attitudes about politics. Political communication is also a means of resocialisation, and was important, for instance, in the re-education policies of the occupation Governments. It was not sufficient to make political structures democratic in form; the public had to acquire democratic orientations towards politics as well. Since 1945, and in contrast to the hostility towards the regime displayed by major newspapers in the Weimar Republic, there has been a large degree of general support for the Bonn regime by the Press and the broadcasting media

[11] See below, Chapter 9.

which has filtered through to the public, reinforcing support by the population even if such support has not been reflected in political activism. Television, in particular, has also been a means by which the public has been informed about Germany's past, especially through programmes on the Weimar and Hitler periods, and has thus, to some extent, enabled both the older and the younger generations of voters to come to terms with that past.

Finally, as Karl Deutsch has demonstrated,[12] political communication is closely associated with political integration. This is shown very clearly in Germany, where the division of what was formerly one society and one culture has led, in East and West Germany, to the development of two distinct cultures, the utilisation of separate mass-media networks, the growth of different political vocabularies and, as a consequence, a strengthening of the cohesion of the two separate polities: the German Federal Republic (BRD) and the German Democratic Republic (DDR).

In West Germany, political integration at the national level is fostered by the mass media, through nation-wide television programmes, the reporting of national news in the Press (often the same agency report will provide the headline story in many of the major regional newspapers) and by the existence of national parties and pressure-groups as channels of communication between the people and the Government. Countering this tendency towards national integration are the forces making for regional identification, such as the localised basis of newspaper production and circulation, their concentration on local news, regional television news programmes, the considerable responsibilities of *Land* Governments, particularly for education, and the sense of pride in the historical traditions of *Länder* such as Hamburg and Bremen, Hesse, the Saarland and Bavaria, which was a monarchy until 1918 and which not only has the most highly developed sense of local identification of all the *Länder*, but the most distinctive regional culture and dialect to accompany it.

CONCLUSION

In the broadest sense, the whole of politics may be viewed as communication: parliamentary debates, election speeches,

[12] K. Deutsch, *Nationalism and Social Communication* (New York, 1953).

committee discussions, conspiracies, threats, bargaining and so forth. More particularly, though, political communication is a significant, though often neglected, aspect of the political process, and the structural pattern, the quality and the survival of the system are affected by it. This chapter has shown how, on the one hand, political communication in West Germany is carried on by methods very similar to those of other industrial societies, but, on the other hand, how important are the historical factors inhibiting certain types of media usage, and how sensitive still are questions of ownership and control, especially where the Federal Government is involved.

8 Conflict, Co-operation and Development

THE FUNCTIONS OF THE POLITICAL SYSTEM

The political system provides the means of converting the demands of the public into policy outputs. But it has other functions in addition. It is the arena within which certain types of conflicts are pursued and resolved; it is an instrument for achieving consensus and co-operation among the various groups and interests within the community; and the political system offers one of the most important of the ways in which a society can adapt to changes in its environment and develop new capacities. Not every political system performs these functions effectively or even adequately. The West German political system is open to criticism on several grounds with regard to all three functions. But, by and large, it does seem to be achieving something more than a 'survival quality' in coping with the conflicts which exist in West German society, in the encouragement of co-operation and in aiding the adaptation of West Germany to its new role in a changing world.

POLITICS AND CONFLICT

Conflict in political life arises from the many diversities which exist among the individuals and the groups within a political system. People possess different values and different ideologies, they have different needs and different interests. There are three basic strategies which polities may adopt for dealing with political conflict: they may attempt to depoliticise conflict, by refusing to resolve it, or by allowing or encouraging other social agencies – the economy, the military, social stratification, the churches – to act as arbiters. Or a polity may settle conflicts authoritatively by decree. This is the strategy associated with despotisms, whether benevolent or not, with dictatorships, with totalitarian rule, and is the strategy of which Germany has had most experience. Or the polity may seek to accommodate conflict, by devising rules and procedures within which conflicts may be settled by discussion, voting, bargaining and other means associated with parliamentary and democratic government.

In West Germany there are many sources of political conflict. Among the most obvious are ideological differences (some of which form the basis of political party programmes); differences of social class and of economic interest: employer and employee, large and small undertakings, exporting and non-exporting industries, manufacturing and agriculture; the 'generation gap', or, rather, the 'generation gaps' in the plural, for there are three clearly identifiable political generations: the young voters under about thirty years old, the 'war generation' who grew up in the Third *Reich* and recall the war and the occupation which followed, and the older generation who were adults in 1940, and who have memories of Weimar politics as well as of Hitler; to these can be added religious differences, regional divisions, the urban–rural differences and educational distinctions, and already the list is long. In addition, there are the 'pragmatic' differences of opinion that arise on specific issues, and which are not necessarily related to any sort of relatively permanent traits or attributes, but which may be important in a political controversy.

> Whenever opposing interests meet in German society, there is a tendency to seek authoritative and substantive rather than tentative and formal solutions. Many institutions of German society have been and are still set up in such a way as to imply that somebody or some group of people is 'the most objective authority in the world', and is therefore capable of finding ultimate solutions for all issues and conflicts. In this manner, conflict is not regulated, but 'solved' . . .[1]

This tendency to resolve rather than accommodate political conflict, to rely on authoritative decisions as final and infallible rather than temporary and flexible, still persists in West German politics. But since 1945 tendencies have developed towards the encouragement of diversity and the recognition of the existence of differing interests in politics. Although Adenauer seemed to view his own policies and de-

[1] Dahrendorf, *Society and Democracy in Germany*, p. 137.

cisions as infallible, and Schumacher, the first leader of the Social Democrats after the war, was also inclined to intolerance of opposition within or outside his party,[2] the political parties have more recently come increasingly to incorporate and accommodate a diversity of views within their own ranks. Sometimes this has not been a happy accommodation: the FDP in particular is still a very uneasy coalition of right-wing and progressive elements. But the SPD since the Godesberg Programme, the CDU–CSU with such political leaders as Kiesinger and Katzer, Kohl and Strauss within their organisation, have both learned to live with, and indeed to benefit from, diversity and internal conflict. Competition among the parties has itself come to be viewed more generally as one of the arenas of political conflict, and not (as was alleged by enemies of parliamentary democracy in the Weimar period, for instance) as a vehicle for furthering the anti-social and self-seeking purposes of groups which put their own interests before those of the nation. The federal structure of the state has also provided an institutionalised arena for conflict. Federation may not in itself be a guarantee of democracy, but it does constitute a barrier to the development of totalitarianism, as Hitler well recognised by his centralisation policies. The *Bundestag* provides the major opportunities for political conflict to find expression: among the parties, between the Government and the legislature, even between generations. Debates, committee work, motions of no confidence, various types of parliamentary question: these are the formal opportunities for opposition in the *Bundestag*, though it is important not to equate these institutions directly with those of Britain or the United States, for instance. One writer has pointed out, for example, that 'The oral question remains by and large in the realm of the backbencher's title to recognition; it becomes an auxiliary weapon for political criticism only on special occasions.'[3] Among such occasions have been controversies concerning rearmament, the *Spiegel* affair and foreign policy. The institutionalisation of opposition and, in 1969, the change of Government, are both significant improvements in the 'conflict management' of the Federal Re-

[2] L. Edinger, *Kurt Schumacher* (Stanford, 1965) esp. pp. 126–37, 167–73.

[3] O. Kirchheimer, 'Germany: The Vanishing Opposition', in R. Dahl (ed.), *Political Oppositions in Western Democracies* (New Haven, 1966) p. 256.

public. True, the Grand Coalition seemed to be a set-back to such improvement and encouraged the growth of extra-parliamentary opposition, but this proved to be only temporary. The mass media are also free to play an opposition role, whether that of the Springer Press denouncing the *Ostpolitik* of Brandt's coalition, *Der Spiegel* attacking the policies of the Grand Coalition, or the magazine programmes of the television networks probing the consequences of current policy on all manner of issues. Such publicity would once have been criticised as improper, even near-treasonable, but it is now more positively valued as a necessary part of democratic politics.

A distinction may be drawn between opposition based on clear-cut alternative policy programmes, and opposition centred on the struggle for office. Opposition in Britain may be taken as an example of the first, and the party struggle in the United States as an instance of the second, of these types. In West Germany, at first a combination of circumstances, personality differences and party ideologies encouraged the development of opposition based on quite distinctive alternative party policies. Adenauer regarded Schumacher (the SPD leader) not just as a rival for office, but as the leader of a party whose ideologies and policies were pernicious, dangerous to the survival of the new Republic. In turn, Schumacher viewed Adenauer as the 'Chancellor of the Allies', blind to the true interests of Germany. On foreign policy issues in particular the differences between the Government and the opposition were sharply marked. But under the leadership of Ollenhauer and then Brandt, with the acceptance by the party of the Godesberg Programme, with the recognition by the Social Democrats that the cold war would constrain West Germany's own policies, with the revival of the West German economy encouraging the acceptance of a mixed economic structure, and with their taste for office encouraged by experiences of governing at *Land* and local levels, the SPD more and more came to present an image of an alternative Government, but less the appearance of possessing any clear-cut alternative programme. Such a change has been, to some extent, typical of all Western industrial societies.[4] But the reduction both in class and religious cleavages has been particularly remarkable in West German politics. The Grand Coalition experience

[4] Ibid., pp. 246–7.

brought the parties by 1969 very close to the American model of competition between leaders and teams, between different orientations towards reform, but with less and less in the way of distinctive substantive policy alternatives. The *Ostpolitik* of the Brandt Government was foreshadowed by the policies of Kiesinger (Brandt, of course, was then Foreign Minister);[5] the CDU has not rejected recent demands for a wider co-determination law, it has only discussed ways of making this proposal congruent with its other policies; both parties have similarly positive attitudes towards the development of education, the improvement of social security provision, the maintenance of West Germany's international linkages and many other political questions.

This situation has encouraged the growth of extra-parliamentary opposition, both in the form of party organisation (the NPD, the revived Communist Party and the breakaway National Liberal Action are the major examples) and as non-party groups concerned with radical reform or even revolutionary change – the students, the ultra-left-wing movements, etc. The provisions of the Basic Law are a constraint on the extent to which 'opposition of principle'[6] can develop (the bans imposed on the Communist Party and Socialist Reich Party illustrate this). In any case, the change of Government in 1969 has meant that an experienced, even vigorous, party is now in opposition for the first time in its history. This, coupled with the new self-confidence of the SPD, has encouraged a return to more clearly differentiated policy positions. Extra-parliamentary opposition still exists; it has almost become a political institution in itself. But its opportunities and the publicity given to it by the mass media have both been reduced since the dissolution of the Grand Coalition.

As in many other states, the courts in West Germany are convenient arenas for the accommodation and settlement of conflict on political, as well as on other, matters. Apart from occasional cases in the civil and criminal courts which possess some consequential political significance, such as certain prosecutions of war criminals, or the case brought against a

[5] See below, Chapter 11.

[6] Kirchheimer, in Dahl (ed.), *Political Oppositions in Western Democracies*, p. 237, defines opposition of principle as 'the desire for a degree of goal displacement incompatible with the constitutional requirements of a given system'.

member of the NPD on charges of wounding arising out of an incident in the 1969 election campaign, the Federal and *Land* Constitutional Courts and the local, regional and Federal Administrative Courts are the institutions which regularly deal with matters involving political conflict. The Constitutional Courts were set up after the war, to issue authoritative interpretations of *Land* constitutions and the Basic Law, and, in doing so, to provide one of the 'checks and balances' to executive power so conspicuously lacking in the Weimar regime. The Federal Constitutional Court corresponds in many respects to the American Supreme Court. It has powers of judicial review of governmental actions; it is bound only by the Basic Law; it is empowered to resolve conflicts between the federal and *Land* levels of government, as well as between the legislative and executive branches of the Federal Government itself. However, in West Germany the Court can, unlike the Supreme Court, give advisory decisions on issues which do not necessarily take the form of *bona fide* cases. It is building up a substantial body of case law on matters such as the boundaries of federal authority, the 'democratic' nature of political parties, and the definition and defence of the civil liberties of individuals and groups against encroachment by the Government.[7] It has sixteen members, sitting as two courts for division of work. Six of the members are chosen from the ranks of the judicial profession, and have life tenure. The other ten serve eight-year terms only, and come from non-judicial sources: the civil service, major interest-groups, the political parties, etc. Unlike the American Supreme Court, verdicts are given from the bench as a whole, and dissenting opinions are not published. The Court meets in Karlsruhe.

CO-OPERATION AND CO-ORDINATION

The need for co-operation and co-ordination in politics is independent of the problem of dealing with conflict. Even if it were conceivable that all political conflicts should somehow be resolved, the need to co-ordinate the activities of the various agencies and levels of government, and of the multiplicity of political groups, organisations and institutions, would remain. In addition, the need for a degree of general consensus

[7] C. Foster and G. Stambuk, 'Judicial Protection of Civil Liberties in Germany', *Political Studies*, IV 2 (June 1956) 190–4.

on procedures as well as on outcomes is also required, for it is this fundamental consensus that provides support for the continued existence of the system and the regime. In West Germany the federal structure and the system of local government are both ways in which arrangements have been made for the achievement of co-ordination, co-operation and consensus.

Germany has a long history of federalism. In the Second *Reich* the federal pattern was the instrument by which Germany was able to achieve unification, and by which it was held together once unification was completed. It allowed Bavaria, for instance, to co-exist with Prussia – a major achievement indeed! Though federalism was seriously diluted in the thirty years between the end of the First World War and the creation of the Bonn Republic, in 1949, as a result of the deliberations of the Parliamentary Council, the new regime was organised on the basis of relatively strong *Land* responsibilities. Here the political influence of the *Länder* on the constitutional structure was asserted with effect. They had been in existence as working entities with governmental structures for several years prior to the creation of the new Republic, and were determined to surrender as little of their responsibility as possible to the central Government. The form of federation is somewhat unusual. Under the Basic Law, the Federal Government and the *Bundestag* have strong legislative powers (though the *Bundesrat* has a significant role in the legislative process also), but administratively they rely very much on the *Länder* Governments. This means that considerable co-operation and co-ordination is necessary to implement legislation. The Federal Government does possess limited supervisory powers over *Land* administration of federal programmes: through investigatory powers, even the use of judicial or military force *in extremis*; but, so far, the Federal Government has relied on the directives it issues concerning the administration of certain federal laws, and on political negotiation on an *ad hoc* basis.[8]

The division of responsibilities between the federal and *Land* authorities means that on certain matters forms of co-operation must be found to produce a satisfactorily co-

[8] K. Neunreither, 'Federalism and West German Bureaucracy', *Political Studies*, VII 3 (Oct. 1959) 232–45.

ordinated policy. To take one example: the proposal to create a Science Council (*Wissenschaftsrat*) in 1957 a treaty-like agreement signed by the *Länder* Governments and the Federal Government. The standing conferences of *Länder* ministers (such as the Education Ministers' conference) another very effective co-ordinating device.

Recently, doubt has been expressed about the suitability of the current *Länder* divisions for coping with the very important, often costly and far-reaching political responsibilities with which they must be concerned. Two aspects of *Länder* divisions in particular are generally mentioned in this respect: the very large differences in population and, to a lesser extent, in area, among the *Länder*, and their relative wealth. This latter point is particularly sensitive to those *Länder* which, by means of equalisation payments, subsidise their less well-endowed neighbours.[9] North Rhine-Westphalia, Bavaria and Baden-Württemberg may be suitable units for the provision of educational, police, planning and other services. It is more doubtful whether what seem suitable responsibilities for them can also be properly administered by smaller *Länder* such as Bremen, Schleswig-Holstein and Saarland. Several plans for reform of *Land* boundaries have been suggested. Most of these involve some merging of the four northernmost *Länder*: Schleswig-Holstein with Hamburg, Bremen with Lower Saxony, or even all four as a single *Land*; the preservation unchanged of North Rhine-Westphalia and Bavaria, perhaps also of Baden-Württemberg; and merging of Hesse with Saarland and Rhineland-Pfalz. Though the Luther Commission reported on reform of the *Länder* in 1955, change since then in terms of such factors as population shifts, industrial location and the progress of the Common Market seems to indicate the need for a new expert commission to examine the question. Two political factors must also be mentioned: first, as the 1970 referendum over the division of Baden from Württemberg showed, there is still considerable lingering affection for certain formerly autonomous areas which would make itself felt in, for instance, Hamburg, Bremen and Saar-

[9] *Der Spiegel*, 14 Sept. 1970, in an article 'Sprache der Bremser', showed that in 1969 Baden-Württemberg, Hesse, Hamburg and North Rhine-Westphalia transferred a total of 1,885 million DM to other *Länder*, ranging from Bremen (receiving 30 million DM) to Lower Saxony (receiving 649 million DM).

land if plans were accepted for their absorption into other *Länder*; secondly, the actual redistribution of *Länder* will, under the present constraints of the Basic Law, affect party control in the *Bundesrat*. The SPD majority in Hesse might swamp the other parties' votes in Saarland and Rhineland-Pfalz. The Hamburg and Bremen SPD majorities might guarantee an SPD majority for the new northern *Länder*. So such reform will be a political, as well as an administrative, question. Whether the powers, as well as the structure, of the *Länder* will also be reformed is more difficult to foresee. Again, *Land* jealousies will be aroused unanimously at any hint of centralisation tendencies that affect their powers or their finances, but it cannot be claimed that the current divisions of responsibilities between the Federation and the *Länder* are at all satisfactory.

The special role of the *Bundesrat* as an instrument of federalism, as well as a second legislative chamber, must also be emphasised. The *Bundesrat* was not designed solely as a means of providing a check to the legislative powers of the *Bundestag*. It was also given the very positive function of allowing the *Länder* the opportunity of safeguarding their rights when these appeared threatened by federal legislation, and, by allowing the *Länder* representatives to scrutinise legislation for the administration of which they might well be responsible, to improve and amend such legislation so that it could be implemented more practicably. The fact that *Land* civil servants, rather than ministers, perform the greater part of the committee work of the *Bundesrat* – often the most crucial of the stages of the legislative process in that chamber – is indicative of the tendency of the *Bundesrat* to apply bureaucratic criteria to its legislation under consideration. Of course, party considerations do enter into the decisions taken by the *Bundesrat,* but not exclusively so. *Land* interests are also important, and these include ensuring that legislation which the *Länder* must implement is workable administratively.[10] In fact, 'the *Bundesrat* is in a unique position to bridge the gap which twentieth-century critics believe to exist between accredited policy-makers and those who actually

[10] E. Pinney, *Federalism, Bureaucracy and Party Politics in Western Germany: The Role of the Bundesrat* (Chapel Hill, N.C., 1963) esp. chap. v, 'Federalism'.

make policy by administration'.[11] Proposals have been made to reduce the influence of the *Bundesrat* on all legislation except that which clearly concerns *Land* interests, and to give a proportionately greater voice to the more populated *Länder*.[12] Others, especially in Bavaria and the smaller *Länder*, would preserve the present system on the grounds of its special contribution to co-operative, rather than separative, federalism, and its protection of regional minority interests.[13]

The governmental systems of the *Länder* and the local communities are themselves an important part of the co-operative arrangements for dealing with political matters in the Federal Republic. The *Länder* all possess a legislature (with the exception of Bavaria, all unicameral in form), elected at four-yearly intervals (five-year intervals in Saarland) following election campaigns that are growing increasingly intense and increasingly national in orientation. The electoral systems vary from *Land* to *Land*, but all are to a large extent proportional representation systems.[14] They also have Governments arranged more on the style of an American state than a British county council. In North Rhine-Westphalia, for example, besides the Minister-President (the 'Prime Minister' or 'Governor' of the *Land*) there are ministers concerned with the interior (including the police, the *Land* public service, and protection of the constitution), finance, economics and transport, justice, agriculture and forestry, public works and building, social welfare, education and cultural questions, and a ministerial representative to the Federal Government. The *Länder* parliaments do not sit continuously in session, as does the *Bundestag*. None the less, the work is demanding, involving plenary sessions and committee work, and on this account certain types of occupation such as the 'free professions', academic and other public service employment,

[11] E. Pinney, 'Latent and Manifest Bureaucracy in the West German Parliament: The Case of the Bundesrat', *Midwest Journal of Political Science*, VI 2 (May 1962) 164.

[12] See, for example, the article by Alfred Kubel, 'Kein separativer Föderalismus . . .', *Die Zeit*, 12 July 1968.

[13] See articles by Franz Heubl, 'Verteidigung des Föderalismus', *Die Zeit*, 19 July 1968, and Ernst Heinsen, 'Separativer Föderalismus', ibid., 9 Aug. 1968.

[14] R. J. C. Preece, *Land Elections in the German Federal Republic* (London, 1968) chap. iii, '*Land* Electoral Systems', discusses many of the details of the systems in use.

or some types of commercial work, are most compatible with the role of *Landtag* deputy. Indeed, any future reorganisation of *Länder* boundaries and functions might, by enlarging the *Länder*, hasten the introduction of the full-time *Land* deputy.

Local government in West Germany is structurally complex and varied. As in Britain, the basic unit is the county (*Kreis*) or city with county status. Within the county there are town and village councils. In some *Länder* there are also districts, composed of several counties, but these are for purposes of delegation of *Land* responsibilities, and are not autonomous units of local government. The relationships between these units, and between the elected mayor (or lord mayor) and his council, vary from *Land* to *Land*, partly as a result of historical forces, including different practices in the various zones of occupation after the war. In some *Länder*, such as Bavaria, the mayor of a city is elected directly and may serve on a full-time basis (the Lord Mayor of Munich, Dr Hans-Jochen Vogel, is a well-known example). In others, such as North Rhine-Westphalia, the mayor is elected by the town or city council, and is not usually a full-time officer, full-time direction of the administration being in the hands of a chief civil servant. In the rural districts, the equivalent of the mayor, or chairman of the county council as in Britain, is the *Landrat*, generally elected by the council (*Kreistag*), though in some areas he is an appointed official. The size of local government units also varies widely. Several have fewer than a hundred inhabitants, most have fewer than two thousand, yet some have populations larger than half a million. Though the functions of local government are restricted in the main to the provision of services and facilities directly concerned with the local community, such as local transport services, parks and swimming-pools, libraries and public utilities, their elections are watched closely by the parties as being indicative of national trends of opinion, especially as there are no by-elections in West Germany to provide a barometer of levels of public support for the parties between *Land* and federal elections. The tasks of local government are to a large extent the result of delegation (and paid for out of delegated revenues) from the *Land* and Federal Governments. Once again the intertwining of responsibilities and functions demonstrates the need for co-operation and co-ordination in the political system of West Germany.

West Berlin is a special case. Though regarded for some purposes as a city-state *Land*, similar to Hamburg or Bremen, because of its status as an occupied territory the provisions of the Basic Law are suspended in so far as they would apply to Berlin. It sends non-voting observers to the *Bundestag* and *Bundesrat*. But for many purposes it is dealt with by the Federal Government directly, or through the occupation powers. To emphasise the claim of the Federal Republic to West Berlin, various official and party functions take place there on occasion, such as the election of the President in 1969, sessions of the *Bundestag*, and party conferences. The national parties have organisations in West Berlin, and elections for the city council take place on party lines. The legislature is elected for a four-year period, and this body in turn elects the lord mayor, his deputy and the Cabinet of ministers. Special federal grants are made to West Berlin on account of its political importance and in recognition of the economic handicaps it possesses.

POLITICAL DEVELOPMENT AND POLITICAL REFORM

Political development is not just a process associated with new states. It is a mode of political change which may be found in any political system. Though there is dispute about just what constitutes political development, there is general agreement that it is associated with the increase in the capacity of the political system to deal with problems and respond to stress from its environment, with flexibility of government, and the alteration of political structures to forms more suitable to the efficient performance of political functions. A political system, in fact, has only this choice: to be adaptive, or to 'go under' as some states have done in the past, to disappear as a result of fusion or fission, by cession, conquest, internal collapse or other cause.

A number of policy areas which significantly concern the ability of the German Federal Republic to adapt and develop in these terms are treated in Chapter 11 below. Generally, the political system appears to be managing better than ever before to accommodate conflict, and even to make constructive use of conflict when it occurs. A number of political and social reforms which have either been put into effect (such as the lowering of the voting age) or are foreshadowed in the 1969 Government Declaration would not have been politically feasible even ten years ago. New ideas have been put forward to influence political thinking, and many of these have originated from, for example, the student movement, inner-party opposition groups, or the anti-conservative communications media. The reappearance of a strong and relatively cohesive parliamentary opposition may be expected to improve the critical examination, the liveliness and eventually the operative quality of governmental policy. More explicit attention is being given to the need for co-operation among the various levels of government and co-ordination of the several agencies of government involved in policy areas. One example of this is the new 'North German Parliament', a conference of members from all parties represented in the Bremen, Hamburg, Lower Saxony and Schleswig-Holstein *Land* legislatures, which met for the first time in Hanover in October 1970.[15] Another example is the introduction of Parliamentary Secretaries of State into the ministerial structure, in seven departments in 1967, then in all fifteen ministries after the formation of the Brandt–Scheel coalition. This new office is intended to reduce the work-load of members of the Cabinet, and serve as a preparing-ground for those members of the parliamentary party considered to be likely future ministers. The merging of certain departments by the new coalition increased the need for such assistance.[16] The policy-planning staff in the *Kanzleramt*, the conferences of *Land* and federal ministries on specific policy topics or in broad fields such as finance and education, the rationalisation of the departmental structure by Brandt, the efforts by the Federal Government to set broad guidelines for the *Länder* in certain policy areas such as university education: all these are also indicative of an increasing adaptive capacity of the system. The problems of preserving democratic procedures and avoiding the introduction of a federally dominated and technocratic 'administrative state' are very real, but they are recognised, and to

[15] *Die Welt*, 21 Sept. 1970.

[16] F. K. Fromme, 'Die Parlamentarischen Staatsekretäre: Entwicklung der 6 Wahlperiode', *Zeitschrift für Parlamentsfragen*, I 1 (June 1970) 53–83.

date these fears reflect anxiety about the future rather than criticism of the present state of affairs.

Adaptiveness is demonstrated also in the increased flexibility evident in several areas of political life. Old practices and old ideologies are being eroded: in the civil service, the armed forces, the political parties, the *Bundestag* itself, for instance. New and quite radical changes of direction are observable in certain policy areas: labour relations, the *Ostpolitik,* education, taxation, social security. Most significant in this respect, however, are the reforms which have been considered, and in some cases adopted, in the political institutions and processes of the Federal Republic, for change and adaptation in these are preconditions to more flexible policies in other areas. Though the majority system of election was not introduced by the Grand Coalition, the voting age has been reduced, providing opportunities for the political energies of the eighteen- to twenty-one-year-olds to be geared to the political issues and conflicts of the day in a more effective manner. The organisation, functions, campaign methods and finances of the parties are subject to closer public scrutiny than in the Anglo-Saxon democracies, for instance. Parliamentary reform is increasingly a matter for discussion and debate.[17] The federal structure is under review. The Government Declaration of Brandt devoted a complete section to reform policies, including the reduction in the number of ministries, the structure of the Chancellor's Department, the supervisory functions of the *Bundestag,* the creation of a committee for reform of the structure of the Federation, and reform of the public service. Indeed, proposals have been made that the 'provisional' Basic Law itself should be the subject of thorough revision, to shape from it a more permanent constitution, compatible with the very different conditions which exist in Germany, Europe and the international community today compared with those prevailing in 1949.[18]

[17] For examples, see H. Flohr, *Parteiprogramme in der Demokratie* (Göttingen, 1969) esp. pp. 150–1; Olaf von Wrangel, 'Ohnmacht des Abgeordneten', *Die Zeit,* 30 May 1969; and the series 'Krise der Demokratie', ibid., 15 Dec. 1967–2 Feb. 1968 inclusive, especially the articles by R. Dahrendorf (15 Dec. 1967) and E. Kogon (26 Jan. 1968).

[18] *Die Zeit,* 27 Feb. 1970: 'Ist unsere Verfassung tabu?'

PART THREE
The Political Culture

9 Political Culture and Political Behaviour

POLITICAL BEHAVIOUR

Political behaviour is the third of the factors which must be considered in understanding and explaining the politics of West Germany. It interacts with other factors of history and the political system, shaping them and being shaped by them. But 'political behaviour' is a vague term in itself. More precisely, it includes the ways in which people act politically, and the reasons why they act in those ways, in terms of their motivations and values, and the political culture which is the setting for their political ideas and activities.

The focus on political behaviour is therefore different from that which seeks to analyse and describe the political system, its structures and processes. Of course, the system can be described as the sum of all the political behaviour that occurs within it, but while political behaviour can take a wide variety of forms, and can be the result of a large range of different motivations, the system must be studied mainly in terms of pattern aggregates of regular behaviour. The study of political behaviour, however, seeks to understand the variations and irregularities which occur, as well as the regularities, and is interested in the reasons why behaviour takes the form it does. The non-voter, as well as the voter, is of interest; anti-authoritarian attitudes as well as supportive attitudes have relevance. Deviant behaviour is at least as interesting as the conformist behaviour of the well-socialised majority.

Political behaviour is not an independent factor, however. It is affected by the personality of the individual, the social structures and the processes which comprise his society, and the political culture into which he is socialised from his first entry into that society – as an infant, a refugee or a migrant. The political culture consists of the norms and values concerning politics which are prevalent in the political system. In turn, these are the product of historical experience, and more clearly so in West Germany than in any other Western state. The different political cultures of the Bismarckian Empire, the Weimar Republic, the Third *Reich* and the occupation zones after the Second World War were all in sharp contrast to each other. All have contributed to the political culture of present-day West Germany, but the very thoroughness of change in each case itself indicates an underlying adaptive quality of that political culture at some basic level. Another, and relatively persistent, aspect of German political culture in its various manifestations is the set of broad ideologies which have tended to survive within German political life, even if driven underground at various periods: conservatism and liberalism, political Catholicism, socialism, nationalism and radicalism of the left and the right. These have given a coherence to political discourse over the years, though in turn they have themselves been modified by experience.

THE WEST GERMAN CITIZEN AND THE POLITICAL SYSTEM

A body of formal rules, such as the Basic Law, and a set of institutions, do not in themselves do more than provide a framework of possibilities for political activity. The attitudes of the population towards politics and the political system are important in determining the way in which politics is carried on within a society. The aspects of the relationship between the West German citizen and his political system which are considered here on account of their particular relevance are: his attitudes towards the political community, the regime and its politicians; the political socialisation process; notions of political efficacy; the modes and extent of political participation; and the relationship of women and young people to politics.

In view of the past, and the ease with which the Weimar democracy was permitted to evolve into a totalitarian dictatorship, the question of how firm is the acceptance of the current regime is still of considerable importance even two decades after its foundation. The persistence of right-wing radicalism, the *Spiegel* affair, the formation of the Grand Coalition, the Emergency Laws, student opposition – all these have revived fears that the present democratic regime is only temporary, and that, given the necessary combination of factors, the West German would willingly revert to an authoritarian form of government. On the other hand, there are positive signs of support for the regime to be observed as well. Though the rank order changes, polls show that some 60–70 per cent of the people 'have a good opinion of' many leading politicians.[1] Support for parties of a radical nature is low, and even when such support appears to be increasing (as with the NPD vote during 1967–9) the increase is relatively small and only temporary. Opposition to the democratic order is rarely expressed in any public form (though of course the Basic Law inhibits the formation of anti-democratic parties). The Almond and Verba comparative survey, *The Civic Culture*,[2] contains several indications of the extent of support for the Bonn regime. On the negative side, pride in the political system is low (only 7 per cent of respondents mentioned this in West Germany, compared with 85 per cent in the United States and 46 per cent in the United Kingdom), respondents preferring to mention the 'characteristics of the people' (36 per cent) and the economic system (33 per cent).[3] On the other hand, more of the respondents claimed to follow accounts of political affairs (34 per cent) than in any of the other societies investigated, and the ability to name leading politicians and ministries was also higher than in the other countries.[4] The authors, in their assessment of the West German political culture as one of 'political detachment and subject competence', summarised the attitude of the West German citizen thus: 'Germans tend to be satisfied with the performance of their government, but to lack a more general attachment to the system on the symbolic level.'[5] However, the 'crucial point may not be the fact that there is little deep attachment to the system, but that there is little deep rejection of it.'[6] Certainly there are no signs that this lack of attachment is increasing, nor that on a day-to-day basis the laws passed by the Government are being disobeyed or frus-

[1] *Die Welt*, 13 Nov. 1970.

[2] G. Almond and S. Verba, *The Civic Culture* (Little, Brown edn, Boston, 1965).

[3] Ibid., p. 64.

[4] Ibid., pp. 54, 58.

[5] Ibid., p. 313.

[6] S. Verba, 'Germany: The Remaking of a Political Culture', in L. Pye and S. Verba, *Political Culture and Political Development* (Princeton), 1965) p. 146.

trated. Indeed, one might with justice claim that the West German political system is now less fragile than those of France and Italy, or possibly than the United States.

'For ruling values to be valid, it is not sufficient to write them into party programmes, laws, or even constitutions. Men must get to know the values by which they are supposed to act; they must learn them.'[7] Political socialisation is the process by which a citizen acquires the dominant norms and attitudes of his political culture (or subculture). Such acquisition can be thorough, or it can be weak. For West Germans, socialisation experiences have been complicated by the fundamental and frequent changes of regime, and the different norms and attitudes acceptable in each, of the past sixty years. A seventy-year-old citizen today would have been born and have spent his early youth (the most formative period for socialisation) in the expansive, confident Empire of Wilhelmian Germany. Aged about seventeen, he would have experienced the traumas of defeat, hardship, revolution, the abdication of the Kaiser and the establishment of the Weimar Republic. Aged thirty-two, he would have become a citizen of the Third *Reich*, would probably have served in the armed forces, only to be subject in his mid-forties to another defeat, an occupation regime, de-Nazification and perhaps re-education. Four years after the end of the war, he could have voted for the first *Bundestag* of the Bonn Republic, expected to adjust to a new democratic order in a state divided from the rest of Germany. Given such changes, it is little wonder that doubts are expressed about the ability – let alone the willingness – of the older German citizen to acquire democratic attitudes to politics.

There are many agencies of political socialisation in West German society. The family is usually regarded by many political scientists as perhaps the most important agency of socialisation; it has almost exclusive influence over the pre-school years of the child, and is then a continuing part of his background for the next dozen or so years, years of learning and the acquisition of experience. However, in West Germany, Dahrendorf has postulated that the family has been the agency for the fostering of the 'private virtues', and education the agency for instilling the 'public virtues' – including,

[7] Dahrendorf, *Society and Democracy in Germany*, p. 312.

therefore, the attitudes towards politics.[8] But even accepting the force of this distinction, the traditional authoritarian structure of the German family, the political opinions, experiences and attitudes of the parents (especially the father) and the opportunities afforded within the family for political experiences and the reception of political information (is the television switched off when a political programme is announced?; what newspapers are delivered to the home?; does the family ever discuss politics?) may all be expected to have an effect on the political socialisation of the children. There may be some validity in the view that the German family is becoming liberalised, that both the wife and the children are less under the dominance of the father and that politics is increasingly a matter for discussion openly in the home. But the family as a source of loyalty and the centre of values still has a predominance in West Germany greater than it possesses in Britain or the United States. In addition, the 'shadow of the past' will continue to be a peculiar factor in political socialisation for many years to come, with adolescents questioning their fathers, younger children their grandfathers, about the Hitler period and the war.

The educational system is the second important agency of political socialisation, and much attention was given by the occupation authorities to this aspect of the work of reconstructing German schools. Two things had to be ensured: that the nationalist and racialist teachings of the Nazi period were eliminated from textbooks and lessons alike, and that some explicit teaching of civics and politics was provided. To a large extent, these tasks have been fulfilled under the Bonn regime. True, exaggerated views of the 'other Germany' have crept into books and lessons, but on the whole the West German teenager is given more opportunity of learning, directly and indirectly, about political matters than his predecessors, or his contemporaries in many other European states. But while the modern schoolboy may be relatively well informed about politics, the imitation of student demands for participation in decision-making by schoolchildren (who, in Germany, may be nineteen or twenty years old, and thus of voting age, before they leave) is a sign that socialisation in the schools is perhaps not offering sufficient opportunity for learning atti-

[8] Ibid., p. 313.

tudes of participation and competence, and in any case the persistence of 'dwarf schools'[9] in the rural areas and of church schools, especially in Catholic areas, and the attitudes of many of the older teachers to ideas of participation in politics all militate against the schools being able to act as preparing-grounds for democratic citizenship. The universities are coming to play a more important role, but in view of signs of reaction against student demands for increased participation, and since in any case only a small percentage of school-leavers enter the universities, their quantitative socialising effect may be small in relation to the population as a whole.

Socialisation is a continuing process, though normally its most fundamental effects are achieved during childhood. The influences of the mass media, of primary groups outside the family (e.g. work groups), and membership in voluntary organisations, whether their purpose is political (e.g. parties) or non-political (e.g. churches), can all be important. Given the sudden political changes which have occurred in Germany, and the relatively passive socialisation roles of the family and the schools in the Federal Republic, these other agencies have been more significant than they are in countries where family and educational experiences encourage positive political attitudes and give more opportunities for participation. In particular, the influence of television, with its facility for showing politics to be a constructive, respectable and high-status occupation (as well as, at times, a destructive and violent force) and one in which other people participate with effect, may well have been grossly underestimated as an agency of political socialisation in West Germany in the past decade.

An important product of the socialisation process is the notion of political efficacy. The *Civic Culture* study found that, among West German respondents, while many said that they had the possibility of influencing the outcome of regulations at the local level, only 38 per cent were prepared to say that they could affect the outcomes of the national Government.[10] There are many possible explanations of this low

[9] 'Dwarf schools' (*Zwergschulen*) are schools in small villages where only a few pupils attend, generally representing a wide range of ages, and taught by only one or two teachers.

[10] Almond and Verba, *The Civic Culture*, p. 142.

sense of political efficacy, but the traditional passive role expected of the citizen, the remoteness of national policy-making from the man-in-the-street, and the cataclysmic changes that have occurred in national politics in Germany this century over the heads of the average citizen – wars, inflation, revolutions, war crimes, occupation, partition and so on – are all factors of some relevance.

However reluctantly and however infrequently, the West German citizen does participate in politics at least to the extent of turning out to vote in *Land* and federal elections. Voting turnout is the highest of Western democracies. At-

TABLE 5

Voting Turnout in Certain Western Elections

Election	*Turnout* (per cent)
United States presidential election 1968	61·0
United States congressional elections 1966	49·0
French general election 1968 (first ballot)	80·0
British general election 1970	72·0
West German federal election 1965	86·8
West German federal election 1969	86·7
North Rhine-Westphalia *Land* election 1970	73·6
Hesse *Land* election 1970	82·7
Rhineland-Pfalz *Land* election 1971	79·3

tendance at election meetings is also relatively high. West German political leaders such as Brandt, Strauss, Schiller, Kiesinger and Barzel spoke to large audiences wherever they were billed, whether in city halls, suburban parks or small-town market-places, during the campaign of 1969. Even local candidates can usually attract a sizeable audience in federal and *Land* campaigns. But beyond this, rates of participation fall away rapidly. Membership of political parties or political groups is very low, and of these members, only a small percentage can be called active members or office-holders. Survey research has revealed a low level of party identification,[11] a

[11] M. Kaase, 'Determinanten des Wahlverhaltens bei der Bundestagswahl 1969', *Politische Vierteljahresschrift*, XI 1 (Mar. 1970) 57–60.

general lack of interest in politics[12] and a large number of people who think they should 'only participate passively'.[13]

Two groups of the population are of particular interest in a consideration of political behaviour in West Germany: women and young people. One indication of the extent of change from an authoritarian political style (prevalent in the

TABLE 6

Party Membership in West Germany

SPD	779,000
CDU	300,000
CSU	107,000
FDP	90,000
NPD	30,000
DKP	30,000

Sources: DKP: *Der Spiegel*, 18 Jan. 1971, p. 26; other parties: B. Zeuner, *Innerparteiliche Demokratie* (West Berlin, new ed., 1970). The DKP total is for January 1971, the other figures for the beginning of 1970.

Weimar as well as in the imperial and Nazi periods) to a more democratic style is the progress which has been made in reducing inequality of opportunity in political life as between the sexes, and the elimination of the notion that only adults of mature years should be seen or heard in politics.

Women were first enfranchised in Germany in 1918. However, the prevailing norms in Weimar Germany did not readily accept an active political role for women, and it was due as much to Hitler's policies,[14] and the exigencies of the Second World War (in which women perforce had to undertake several unfamiliar roles), plus the democratic values imported by the occupation regimes, that women have come to play a more active part in political life in West Germany. Even so,

[12] Ibid., p. 74. In January 1968, 47 per cent, and even in September 1969 (at the height of the federal election campaign) 42 per cent of the voting-age population indicated that they had no interest in politics.

[13] Almond and Verba, *The Civic Culture*, p. 127 (the figure of 38 per cent who agreed that 'one should only participate passively' was the highest of the five countries investigated).

[14] See D. Schoenbaum, *Hitler's Social Revolution* (London, 1967) chap. 6, for the view that Nazi policy towards female emancipation was initially conservative. On the other hand, the general effects of the attacks on traditional social structures in the Third *Reich* did not leave the position of women unaffected.

the distinction between participation of men and women is still marked. Women constitute less than a quarter of party members. Few women ever become members of the Cabinet or hold leading party offices, except in women's organisations, of course, and only a small proportion of candidates (148 at the 1969 federal elections) or elected members of the *Bundestag* or the *Land* parliaments are women.

TABLE 7
Women in Politics

Party membership:	SPD	1965	17·4 per cent
	FDP	1965	7–8 per cent
	CSU	1965	about 5 per cent
	CDU	1964	13·3 per cent
Federal executive committee, CDU 1964			6 (of 69)
Party executive, SPD 1964			5 (of 32)
Delegates to party conference, SPD 1964			29 (of 300)
Members of *Land* parliaments, 1961–5			7·5 per cent
Bundestag 1965: candidacies,	CDU		77 (11 elected)
	SPD		61 (17 elected)
	FDP		33 (2 elected)
	CSU		5 (3 elected)

Note: Of the 33 women elected, only 8 (about 3 per cent of the total directly elected candidates) were elected from constituency rather than list candidacies.
Source: M. Fulles, *Frauen in Partei und Parlament* (Köln, 1969).

Not only is there still this significant gap in the participation rates of men and women in politics (a gap which, in some cases, is at least as large in Britain and the United States, for instance), but the voting behaviour of women is also different. Though the bias lessened at the 1969 election, the proportion of women who vote CDU or CSU is noticeably higher, the proportion voting SPD lower, than the proportion of men who do so.[15] This difference is associated with other factors. More women than men are regular churchgoers (which would incline them to the Christian Union parties anyway); women voters tend to be older, on average, than male voters (almost a third of women voters are over sixty years old); they have had less full-time education, and a larger percentage of women

[15] In 1965, half the women who did vote, voted for the CDU or CSU. Since there are more women than men in the electorate, the effect is amplified to the advantage of the Christian Union parties.

than men are to be found among the less well informed about politics.[16]

Unlike women, whose political importance still seems to be confined to the disproportionate tendency which they have to vote CDU–CSU, the role of young people in politics has become more active and of more general importance since the end of the Second World War. This may be attributable partly to the more explicit nature of the socialisation process to which they have been subjected (see above, p. 119). In part it has been associated with an international trend, especially among students, to greater political involvement on the part of young people. In part, it is also a result of Hitler's attacks on tradition and his politicisation of youth through the Nazi Party. The recent reduction in the voting age from twenty-one to eighteen in federal and most *Land* elections has given more young people the opportunity to vote, and made them a target for party propaganda aimed at winning their first loyalties ('18 votes, 18 counts!' was one of the slogans used on posters in the North Rhine-Westphalia *Landtag* elections in 1970; 'To be able to vote is to be able to change things' was another aimed at the youth vote'). Younger people are being appointed to important public positions in West Germany: Professor Dahrendorf, first to a post at the Foreign Office in 1969 as Parliamentary Secretary, then to an important appointment in West Germany's Common Market representation in 1970; von der Vring, at thirty-three Rector of the new University of Bremen; Hans Apel, the SPD deputy leader of the *Fraktion* in the *Bundestag* – these are just three examples, and the average age of members of the *Bundestag* has fallen considerably as a result of the 1969 elections. A survey of students in 1968 found that over half the respondents were 'strongly' or 'very strongly' interested in politics, and a similar proportion were prepared to regard themselves as supporters of a particular political party, though only 5 per cent were party members. Of those who were not yet party members, about six out of ten considered that they might become members in the future. Though comparatively more young people disagreed with statements about their political inefficacy than did a representative sample of the general population, nevertheless between one-half and two-thirds

[16] See *Der Spiegel*, 1 Sept. 1969, pp. 32–49: 'Wie wahlen die Frauen?'

agreed that they had no influence on what the Government did, or that such influence was limited to elections, and that politics was too complicated to understand properly.[17]

Though the publicity afforded by the mass media to student demonstrations, and the prominence of young people as hecklers and questioners at election meetings, might prompt the observer to assess West German youth as politically active, a closer examination shows that, while there is certainly an active minority, mainly left-wing and mainly students, as a whole the eighteen- to twenty-five-year-olds as a group do not vote in significantly larger numbers than their older counterparts, and while they may play a prominent part in party organisations, party membership among young people is not very high either.[18]

The relationship between the West German citizen and his political system may be summarised by saying that, while 'the ritual of democratic procedure is respected',[19] and though a greater degree of participation and involvement in politics, especially among young people, is increasingly observable, in general politics continues to be regarded as something apart from the day-to-day experiences of the citizen. He is relatively well informed about politics, he is very ready to vote when he sees it as a duty to do so, but the formal democratic structures of the West German political system have not, as yet, been matched by a readiness on the part of the citizen to see politics as an opportunity as well as an obligation.

THE POLITICAL CULTURE OF WEST GERMANY

Political behaviour is affected by the constraints and opportunities of the political system as it exists: the Basic Law, the laws regulating voting, the rules of Parliament, the working practices of civil servants. It is also shaped by ideas of what constitutes proper or acceptable behaviour, what attitudes ought to be held towards politics, politicians and political

[17] R. Wildenmann and M. Kaase, 'Demokratische Einstellung in der Bundesrepublik Deutschland', *Sozialwissenschaftliches Jahrbuch für Politik*, vol. II (Munich, 1971) pp. 252–80.

[18] Membership of the CDU *Junge Union* is about 117,000 (*Die CDU stellt sich vor* (Bonn, 3rd ed., 1970)), and that of the Young Socialists (*Jusos*) about 200,000 (*Der Spiegel*, 1 Mar. 1971, p. 24).

[19] Dahrendorf, *Society and Democracy in Germany*, p. 447.

participation, what is traditionally demanded of the citizen, and so on – in brief, the political culture. The content of the political culture is transferred, as already shown, by processes of political socialisation. While resulting from the history of a nation, the experiences of West Germany show that aspects of a political culture, at least superficially, can also be the product of deliberate creation, whether by a totalitarian dictatorship, occupation Government or a new regime set up with the consent of occupation Governments.[20]

The contemporary political culture of West Germany is the product of three streams of experience. First and most obviously, it is the product of the special historical experiences of the German political community over many years. Much of the political culture of Prussia was imported into the Second *Reich*. The submissive politics of the late nineteenth century, the instability of the Weimar Republic, the 'finger burning' which for many people was the consequence of their participation in politics during the Hitler period, de-Nazification and the two decades of the Bonn Republic have produced norms and values, attitudes and habits, that differentiate West Germany's political culture from those of its neighbours, or from those of its former allies such as Italy and Japan. Associated with its political past has been its process of social development. As Dahrendorf[21] has shown, the family structure, the educational system, the particular roles of the military and the churches are only some of the more obvious social influences on political culture. But West Germany today shares with France and Britain, for instance, its common European past. All the major states of Western Europe experienced somewhat similar paths of national development (if at different times). All were affected by religious divisions in the past. All were to some extent colonising powers, dependent on international trade. All were members of the system of alliances that have caused and avoided wars in recent history. All shared in the development of Western European civilisation, learning and artistic achievement. Now all face a common danger from Russia, and all are linked by a variety of

[20] 'In the past decade-and-a-half, Germany has been faced with the problem of the remaking of a political culture' (Verba, in Pye and Verba, *Political Culture and Political Development*, p. 131).

[21] Dahrendorf, *Society and Democracy in Germany, passim.*

international organisations. This means that there is no great cause for surprise at finding forms of political behaviour in West Germany that resemble those in other European countries. Thirdly, West Germany shares with many of its European neighbours, and with the United States, Japan and a number of other states, a degree of intensive industrialisation which also affects its political culture. The high level of literacy, relatively large proportions of young people at centres of higher education, the widespread ownership of radios and television sets, urbanisation, mass parties and centralised election campaigning, the emancipation of women, the political role of an influential trade union movement, a specialised political bureaucracy, high levels of public expenditure – the list of similarities could be extended indefinitely. So an accurate description of West German political culture would have to incorporate the industrialised, the European, and the distinctively German components.

Many of these components have been mentioned in considering attitudes towards the system and the regime, to participation and efficacy, earlier in this chapter. It is clear that identification with the political system of West Germany is hampered for some people by lingering feelings of regional pride and loyalty (in Bavaria, Hamburg and the Saar, for instance), and, on the other hand, by attachments to the former Germany, now divided, or to the 'lost territories' under Polish or East German control. The sense of patriotism in relation to the Federal Republic is less than it has been towards other regimes in the past, in part because of the soft-pedalling since 1945 of assertions of West Germany's self-importance. Economic prosperity has increased almost without interruption, and the first set-back to the economy after the 'miracle' led to an increase in votes for the radical right-wing party, the NPD, and a ready acceptance of the 'Grand Coalition' – a retreat from politics.

Despite the secondary and passive role of politics in West German society, political symbols and myths still remain. One special set of these can be found in the rhetoric of right-wing nationalism, echoing many of the phrases and slogans of Nazi oratory, concerned with *Volk*, with the Germanic heartland of Europe, with duty and obedience, the benefits of authority and the disadvantages of party politics.[22] But in more general contexts the myths and symbols have less consistency, and are, on the whole, less interwoven with nationalism. The Berlin Wall, the contrast between freedom in West Germany and suppression in East Germany, democracy, legality, peace, the role of West Germany in a united Europe – these are the references which appear in the ceremonial speeches, which preface reports on the West German political system, or which constitute the perorations of party leaders in election campaigns.

And there is always the past as a kind of negative political culture, a return to which must be avoided at all costs. It is this which makes people in West Germany uneasy at the continuation of war-crimes trials. It is this which makes reconciliation between West Germany and the countries of the Warsaw Pact so difficult. It is this which arouses such controversy when the '20 July plot' is mentioned, or an Eichmann brought to justice, when students and NPD stewards clash at election meetings, or when Brandt's war-time emigration is publicly mentioned. An illuminating indication of the public discomfort that exists over the past, and the gap in the continuity of the political tradition of West Germany, is the attachment of names of political figures to streets, bridges and squares in the Federal Republic. All over West Germany there are examples of an Ebertplatz, a Kennedybrücke, or, more recently, a Konrad Adenauer Allee. But, beyond these names, and those of Hindenburg, the dynasties of the more distant past, and some lesser local politicians, few names from the political life of Germany since 1918 are thought to be suitable or acceptable for such public commemoration.

POLITICAL IDEOLOGIES IN WEST GERMANY

Political behaviour and political culture are both influenced by the existence and persistence of generalised sets of values that can be termed 'ideologies'. These give a coherent pattern to the variety of more specific attitudes, opinions and political demands that constitutes the climate of politics for the Government of the day. They provide reference points for the programmes which parties and other political groups devise

[22] See Tauber, *Beyond Eagle and Swastika*, esp. chap. xi, 'The Ideas and Literature of Nationalism'.

in the struggle for power, and they relate ideas on political matters to ideas in economic, social, religious and other arenas of opinion. Some of these ideologies may be relatively short-lived, especially in an articulated form: Nazism is an obvious example in Germany. In any case, even seemingly permanent ideologies tend to be modified by the passage of time: Communism by the increase in the standard of living of the working class; nationalism by the advent of supra-national institutions; Christian Democracy by the decline in church membership and attendance. Yet it is in terms of such broad ideologies that the continuous nature of German politics over the past century can best be appreciated. Whether transmitted from father to son, or acquired elsewhere, whether passed on directly or indirectly as a set of social attitudes (e.g. tolerance and rationalism in the case of liberalism, traditionalism in the case of conservatism, patriotism in the case of nationalism), whether learned over a long period or acquired as the result of a sudden 'conversion' of some kind, these ideologies constitute the base from which more specific opinions are formed and influenced, and hence are the ultimate sources of much of the political conflict identifiable in the political system. Politics is not just a process for reconciling conflict on matters of a temporary nature, a matter of positions taken up pragmatically, by party groups formed for the purpose of taking power after elections. It is a means of adjustment of differences that result from very basic and incompatible ideologies in politics, though the relative influence of these ideologies will vary from period to period. In the Bismarckian period, nationalism, liberalism and conservatism were important. After unification, political Catholicism and socialism provided challenges. In the Weimar period socialism and liberalism were threatened by radicalism of the left and the right, in working alliance at times with conservatism. Today a liberalism–socialism alliance faces competition from a conservative Christian Democracy and the eruption periodically of radicalism of various kinds, while nationalism is still important in relation to foreign policy issues. These beliefs, as well as the social class or religious adherence or personality attributes of the public, help to explain why the West German citizen acts politically as he does.

Liberalism

The earliest of today's ideologies to emerge as politically influential in Germany was liberalism. This was the product of the Enlightenment, the spread of ideas from France during the revolution, and the growth of intellectual and political freedom in the south-western states of Germany in particular. However, during and after 1848, liberalism acquired a romantic, as well as a rationalist, mode, which stimulated nationalist attitudes, and led to the significant part played by liberals in the nationalism of the Frankfurt Assembly,[23] and in the challenge to authoritarianism in the states of Germany. This challenge being unsuccessful, and Germany becoming united in a manner different from that envisaged by the liberal nationalists of 1848, liberalism began its long series of compromises and defeats which mark its course through modern German history. First they had to accept Bismarck, and Prussia's hegemony: 'In the end, after some resistance, but not too unwillingly or ungraciously, most liberals capitulated to Prussia. In return, the latter made minor concessions to the liberals, concessions without which a modern power-state could not have existed but which did not go far enough to transform Prussia into a durable and viable modern society.'[24] Then they compromised in the Weimar period over Germany's defeat and the new democracy, and finally capitulated to Nazism. Since 1945, liberalism has never found a clear voice or purpose in German politics. The Free Democrats have contained elements that have been anything but liberal, and their new course places emphasis in great measure on reform, but not on liberalism. In the 1969 election programme of the FDP the word 'liberal', apart from one minor reference, is entirely absent, and was only rarely to be seen or heard in any of the party's campaign propaganda. On the other hand, politicians of decidedly liberal views are to be found in the other *Bundestag* parties, and outside the parties altogether. But this is an indication that liberalism is no longer, if it has ever been, an ideological base suited to

[23] 'In four months most of the liberals in Frankfurt were converted from liberalism to nationalism' (H. Kohn, *The Mind of Germany* (Papermac ed., London, 1965) p. 143).

[24] Ibid., p. 129.

modern party politics in Germany. It is rather a disposition that can influence the regime itself (the civil liberties of the Basic Law are certainly liberal provisions, for instance) as well as some of the policy positions of parties of the right and the left. Individualism, protection against the improper exercise of power, civil liberties, the rule of law, internationalism – these elements of liberal ideology are not absent from contemporary politics in West Germany but are overlaid by other, cross-cutting issues of greater coherence and more immediate relevance. Only on certain issues – the *Spiegel* affair, the Emergency Laws, denominational schools – is there a salient liberal position.

Conservatism

Conservatism, and its authoritarian variation, also derives from the period of the French Revolution, and was in many respects a reaction to the liberal ideas of the period. The events of 1848 and the unification of Germany under Bismarck made conservatism an ideology of the authoritarian state, rather than, as in other parts of Europe, of the traditional society. Though Bismarck is often regarded as the leading German conservative, he was, in Kohn's words, 'above party and principle',[25] and used the conservatives as he did the other political groupings in the Empire – as elements for manipulation. Germany's defeat in 1918 lost the 'legitimist' conservatives their authoritarian symbols of Emperor and court, but for the 'romantic' conservatives, seeking a revival of some mythical 'Germanic *Reich*', the new regime provided a major opportunity for distinguishing themselves from the legitimists. The rise of Nazism gave these 'romantic' conservatives an organisational base, and Hitler's accession as Chancellor ended any hopes which the traditionalists had of restoring the old imperial order. After the war, conservatism of any type was intermixed with the now-excoriated Nazi creed, and only slowly did it re-emerge, mainly within the CDU–CSU. Radical parties of the right, offering nationalist and *völkisch* ideologies, also appeared (see below) and managed to attract, at least on a short-term basis, some of the supporters of the Weimar conservative parties. But conservatism in the Federal Republic had to recognise the limits imposed by the Basic

[25] Ibid., p. 153.

Law, and by the international situation also, and has had to come to terms with the imperatives of an urbanised, industrialised society in West Germany. Today, conservatism involves the defence of property rights, especially against nationalisation and other forms of state interference, the support of established authority in political, economic and social spheres, adherence to the Christian churches, a reluctance to come to terms with the Eastern bloc countries, especially without clear compensating advantages for West Germany, and a generally cautious attitude to social reform. The centre and right wings of the CDU and CSU, and the disaffected members of the FDP (especially those who became the supporters of the new National Liberal Action), may be regarded as the most conservative elements in contemporary politics in West Germany.

Socialism

Socialism, first in the form of Marxism, then as a social-democratic creed, has a long and influential history in German politics. The decision of Bismarck to continue the exclusion of the rapidly increasing urban working class from influence within the imperial political order, and the persecution to which he submitted working-class movements, had as its consequence a radicalisation of socialism in Germany. It was not surprising, therefore, that the revolutionary socialism of Marx, with its hostility to the bourgeois order, should have greater appeal to the German worker than the reformist socialism that found expression in Fabianism and parliamentary politics in Britain before the First World War. Parliamentary successes, when they came, brought about divisions in the socialist movement in Germany, and the triumph of the revisionist wing was completed when they led the first Weimar Government, and emphasised when they had to suppress the Spartacist rising of the revolutionary socialists in 1919. Never able to secure a majority under the Weimar electoral system, none the less the SPD was the foremost champion of republican democracy, and a target and a victim of radical extremism from the left and the right. Suppressed by Hitler, with many of its most able leaders in exile, imprisoned or killed during the war, the SPD was the only major party to emerge after the war with its former identity and traditions intact. Despite being overshadowed by the CDU in federal politics, it was frequently a governing party at *Land* and community level, and the formation of the Grand Coalition prefaced its 1969 success, when it was able to lead a coalition Government in partnership with the FDP. Its steady increase in the share of the federal vote in elections since 1953 was due in large measure to the adoption of a modern, less ideological stance, which later found expression in the Godesberg Programme of 1959. In this, emphasis was placed less on collectivisation and other traditional socialist policies, and more on a 'humanitarian society' in which each could develop his personality in conditions of freedom and justice and with equal educational opportunity; on the 'welfare state'; on the control and responsibility of public power and the rejection of totalitarianism; on the democratisation of all areas of society and the

TABLE 8

Increase in the Share of the Federal Vote for the SPD
(per cent)

1953	*1957*	*1961*	*1965*	*1969*
28·8	31·8	36·2	39·3	42·7

economy; and on international co-operation. West German socialism is thus, except in its radical minority forms, a socialism that has had to adjust to the existence of a Communist Germany to the east, and the post-war developments in society and the economy at home. Its adaptation to these factors has left it less a socialism that Marx would have recognised, but more a reformist, to some extent even a liberal, movement that seeks, in the words of its 1969 election slogan, to 'create a modern Germany'.

Nationalism

Nationalism, though the temporary ally of other ideologies, has been their worst enemy. Liberalism suffered in 1848, socialism before 1914, and conservatism in the First World War and in the 1930s. As Kohn has pointed out, 'Nationalism, the drive for national power and unity, undermined democracy after 1918 as it had done in 1848'.[26] Even today, nation-

[26] Ibid., p. 306.

alism allied to radicalism (as in the NPD programme) has been denounced as the greatest threat to the stability of the Bonn regime, and more particularly it is an obstacle to the type of settlements Brandt attempted to achieve with his *Ostpolitik* after the 1969 elections. One could, indeed, write the history of modern Germany as a chronicle of the forms and effects of nationalist ideologies. Unification, the consolidation of the *Reich* under Bismarck, Germanophilism and the pan-Germanic movements prior to the First World War, the reaction to the perceived humiliations of defeat and the Treaty of Versailles by the nationalists after 1918, Hitler's appeals for national unity and power, his strategies of expansion, the reunification and refugee issues since 1945 – the list is long. The forms taken by nationalism have been varied. In 1848 it was a movement of liberals; in the Empire it became a feature of romantic conservatism; in the Weimar Republic it was a revanchist and racist ideology; and since the Second World War it has, for various reasons, only been found in any very explicit form among right-wing and generally radical parties. Today its ideas include demands for reunification, for the removal of foreign troops and the restoration of lost territory (even, for some extremists, of territory gained by force up to 1939), the encouragement and indoctrination of patriotic virtues, and the assertion of the vague *völkisch* racism that (in a now-disguised form) still echoes many of the appeals of the Nazis. Examples of this ideology can be found in the election propaganda of the NPD, in the right-wing 'fringe' Press such as the *Nationalzeitung und Soldatenzeitung*, and occasionally, in a restrained form, in the speeches of some members of the CDU and CSU parties.[27]

Radicalism

To consider radicalism as a single ideology, or, indeed, as an ideology at all, is only a classificatory convenience. Rather, it is a disposition, one perhaps to be found as a shared personality characteristic of left- and right-wing radicals (an intolerance of ambiguity, impatience with obstructions, a belief in simple solutions). Yet it is important in that, whether of a left-

[27] For example, the much publicised speech of Karl von und zu Guttenberg, a CSU member of the *Bundestag*, in the German policy debate on 27 May 1970.

wing or a right-wing variety, it is potentially dangerous to the operation, indeed even the very survival, of the existing system of government. The downfall of the Weimar Republic owed much to left-wing radicalism, as well as to Nazism. The Constitutional Court has banned the Communist Party, as well as the Socialist Reich Party. The present radical movements of the left share many of the aims, policies and attitudes of the NPD and other right-wing radical groups. Three of these shared features are: the unsystematic nature of the programmes of radical movements; hostility to the 'bourgeois democracy' and 'big-capital economy' of contemporary Germany; and a utopian search for a satisfactory form of 'community'. To these should be added, for different purposes, hatred of foreign troops and foreign businesses in Germany (especially those of the Americans), and, as in the closing years of Weimar, the need of each other's existence as 'scapegoat' – the students and Communists seeing the NPD as the home of neo-Nazism, the NPD denouncing the left as long-haired, immoral and Bolshevik. Neither form of radicalism has much support today, in terms of votes, membership or finance, but both have a disruptive potential for the future, and both find in the slow, cumbersome and complicated processes of democratic politics much to criticise.

Christianity

Finally, it would be inexcusable to neglect the influence on German politics of Christian ideology in its political modes. The *Kulturkampf*, the importance of the Catholic Centre Party before and after the Second World War, the collaborative and resistance elements of the churches under Hitler, and the multi-denominational Christian Democratic Party that formed after the Second World War – these have been the important emanations of political Christianity. But its more indirect influence has been extensive. The Godesberg Programme of the SPD acknowledges the influence of Christian, as well as of classical and humanist, ideals on the philosophy of modern socialism. The Basic Law contains echoes of Christian ethics and ideals. The churches themselves are important as transmitters of political attitudes, agents of political socialisation, and as interest-groups with regard to certain political issues.[28] West Germany may no longer be a nation of church-attenders, but it is still basically a Christian nation, and the basic values by which political issues are judged and stances assumed are derived to a very great extent from the Christian tradition.

[28] See above, pp. 61–2.

10 Leadership and Elites

POLITICS AND LEADERSHIP

Leadership is one of the most important elements in the political life of states. Not only is it an inevitable product of large-scale political organisation,[1] but leadership style, the qualities of the occupants of leadership positions, the ability of the political system to recruit leaders of high quality, the commitment of leaders to the values of the regime, the distribution of formal and informal leadership positions – these are all factors which political scientists have studied, and which have been discovered as having influence on the survival, development and capacities of the political system. Leadership is also a form of political behaviour, and can be regarded as a particularly interesting and intensive case of political participation and political influence. It offers to its incumbents opportunities for realising their ideals and plans, whether these concern the unification of Germany, the creation of racial hegemony in Europe, the furtherance of socialism, or whatever. Leadership is contextual: it is related to the personality of the leader, to the political culture of the system in which it is exercised, to the institutional structures which exist for the exercise of leadership roles, to the situation in any particular instance. Thus even very powerful leaders soon discover limits to their ability to realise their schemes, in the form of constraints on resources available to them, or restrictions on their influence because of communications problems, differential role expectations on the part of their followers, shortage of time and so forth. Bismarck had to take into account the role of Parliament as it developed after 1871, and the powers of the Kaiser. Hitler's power was limited by a variety of factors in the system of the Third *Reich*.[2] Adenauer and Brandt, so different in their personalities, so unlike in

[1] As suggested by Michels' famous 'iron law of oligarchy'.
[2] E. Peterson, *The Limits of Hitler's Power* (Princeton, 1969).

policies and programmes, still share the similarities of being constrained in their leadership by the Basic Law, the division of Germany, the power of the USSR and the unchangeable Nazi past.

Historically, Germany's leadership and elite groups changed but little until the great upheavals of 1933 and 1945. Before unification, the princes and the aristocracy ruled, unchallenged by counter-elites, within a social system that was, at least at the summit, static and unquestioned. Unification did not change this situation as much as did industrialisation. The political influence of men such as Krupp and Ballin,[3] the shipping magnate, derived from their key positions as controllers of economic resources. But they did not rule. Even the period during the war when Hindenburg and Ludendorff controlled Germany as a military dictatorship was no exception, for they were from the upper class, just as most of the aristocrats were in the military. The formal positions of leadership after 1918 were occupied by 'new men': Ebert, Marx, Müller, Wirth. But the significant fact about the elites in the Weimar Republic is just their close similarity to those of the closing years of the Empire: the aristocracy, the military, the civil service, the gentlemen-intellectuals and the industrialists – these were the groups who still possessed effective political power, who provided many of the second-rank leaders (as well as some in the first rank, such as Hindenburg, Stresemann, Schleicher and von Papen) and who controlled the channels of political communication. Hitler's leadership and the Nazi elite *were* new.[4] Like Hitler himself, many of his leading supporters came from sections of the community which had not before been associated with the exercise of political power: Goebbels, Hess, Bormann, Ley and Rosenberg would have found it difficult to have achieved comparable prominence within the social system of the Weimar Republic. At the same time, Hitler made sure he controlled or removed those groups which formerly had been powerful – the Army, the civil service, the lawyers and professors, the diplomats – even though certain individuals within these groups became his aides, such as Ribbentrop and von Weizsäcker.

[3] L. Cecil, *Albert Ballin, Business and Politics in Imperial Germany, 1888–1918* (Princeton, 1967), esp. chap. iv, 'Prussians and Politicians'.

[4] See above, pp. 21–3.

With the post-war occupation of Germany by the Allied powers, both the Russians and the Western Allied authorities initiated policies involving the removal of what remained of the totalitarian elite and its replacement by a democratically oriented counter-elite. De-Nazification was an important strategy for this purpose, based on a division of Nazis into criminals, tried by courts and tribunals, and accomplices, often punished by withdrawal of rights to certain types of employment or fines. This process in the Western zones was fraught with difficulties, including the administration of questionnaires to millions of Germans, and the practices of on the one hand informing on fellow-citizens for motives of revenge, on the other hand issuing false testimonials to the authorities to cover up for a relative or associate.[5] Even after the founding of the Federal Republic accusations of 'the return of the swastika' and 'back into power' continued to be made,[6] voicing suspicions that de-Nazification as a policy had not succeeded very well. However, though many of the leaders and members of the political elite had not given positive evidence of resistance to Nazism, neither is there much justification for supposing that they had been enthusiastic supporters of the party, and certainly none that they were formerly members of the Nazi elite. The policies of the occupation authorities for reconstruction in their zones depended on the supply of skills and experience only available from people who held jobs which they had also filled under the Nazi regime. This requirement, plus the great difficulties in administering a thorough de-Nazification programme, inevitably resulted in anomalies and compromises. Despite this, the occupation policies in the Western zones did succeed in providing opportunities for political experience and advancement which enabled a democratic elite to emerge by 1949.[7]

[5] C. FitzGibbon, *Denazification* (London, 1969).

[6] See Lord Russell of Liverpool, *The Return of the Swastika* (London, 1968), and A. Horne, *Back into Power* (London, 1955).

[7] This paragraph owes much to the article by L. Edinger, 'Post-totalitarian Leadership: Elites in the German Federal Republic', *American Political Science Review*, LIV 1 (Mar. 1960) 58–82.

POLITICAL LEADERSHIP IN THE FEDERAL REPUBLIC

The three most important formal leadership positions in the Federal Republic are those of the President, the Chancellor and the Minister-President of a *Land*.

TABLE 9

Presidents and Chancellors of the Federal Republic

Presidents		*Chancellors*	
Theodor Heuss	1949–59	Konrad Adenauer (CDU)	1949–63
Heinrich Lübke	1959–69	Ludwig Erhard (CDU)	1963–6
Gustav Heinemann	1969–	Kurt-Georg Kiesinger (CDU)	1966–9
		Willy Brandt (SPD)	1969–

The three Federal Presidents, Heuss, Lübke and Heinemann, have all possessed very different personalities, and their periods of office have coincided with very different periods in the history of the Federal Republic. Heuss, a liberal intellectual, presided over the critical first decade of the Bonn Republic. His restrained style of leadership was in keeping with the intentions of the 'founding fathers', who had wished to avoid a politically powerful presidential office. This restraint was partly responsible for the way in which Adenauer was able to build up the powers of the Chancellorship. However, when Adenauer came to consider the possibility of himself succeeding Heuss, and enlarging the political position of the President, it was too late. Constitutionally and practically, Heuss had established the Presidency as a type of 'constitutional monarchy', with ceremonial and symbolic powers, with a certain right to influence, but not to control, the actions of the Government. Lübke did not seek to add to the leadership powers of the Presidency, and seemed content to allow Adenauer, Erhard and Kiesinger to centre political attention on the Chancellorship. Heinemann, in the first years of his term, while not going beyond the previous limits of his office, has given indications that he regards it as a position of opportunity for national leadership. He himself emphasised in his inaugural address (1 July 1969) that the pursuit of peace would be his first obligation, and in an earlier interview[8] he said that, as well as being the representative of the state, he saw the President as having the task of concerning himself with the

[8] *Die Welt*, 30 June 1969.

everyday needs, thoughts and opinions of the people, as a President of the people (*Bürgerpräsident*) as much as a President of the state. The television broadcast which he made in 1970 to commemorate the twenty-fifth anniversary of the end of the Second World War was one example of this more positive interpretation of his role.

The office of Federal Chancellor has also been occupied by four contrasting personalities. Adenauer's period in office gave rise to the phrase 'Chancellor democracy', though this 'may simply be another description for the Adenauer Era'.[9] It would be excessive to describe Adenauer as a charismatic leader, but his personality, the fact that he was the *first* Chancellor of the new Republic, and his long unbroken occupancy of the office all combined to make the term 'Chancellor' synonymous with *Der Alte* ('the old one'). Thus Erhard was handicapped by his very different, and far less effective, leadership style, by his failure to overcome crises as Adenauer had appeared able to do, by the initial retention by Adenauer of the chairmanship of the party, and by the simple fact that people found it difficult to accept a Chancellor who so obviously was not Adenauer. Kiesinger, Erhard's successor, on the other hand, did have the great advantage of physical similarity to Adenauer, and the 1969 CDU electoral campaign quite clearly tried to take advantage of this. Brandt's style is different again. It is more urgent, more aggressive than any of his predecessors, and is associated with his former offices of Mayor of Berlin and Foreign Minister, as well as his length of occupancy of the leadership of his party. But, as with the Presidency, it is too early to make any broad general assessment of the type of leadership that the Chancellorship requires or permits. The period since 1949 has been so full of changes, political, economic and international, that each of the incumbents has necessarily presented a different type of leadership in part, at least, as a response to the circumstances of the time.

In the *Länder,* the office of Minister-President has offered a variety of opportunities for political leadership. Clearly, there is a great difference in the type of leadership required to govern, say, Bavaria or North Rhine-Westphalia as contrasted

[9] F. Ridley, 'Chancellor Government as a Political System and the German Constitution', *Parliamentary Affairs,* XIX 4 (June 1966) 460.

with Bremen or Schleswig-Holstein. Yet many politicians have made reputations as political leaders in the office of Minister-President, Kiesinger (Baden-Württemberg), Kohl (Rhineland-Pfalz), Zinn (Hesse) among them. Stoltenberg, a leading member of the CDU, left Bonn politics to seek the Minister-Presidency of Schleswig-Holstein in 1971. Kuhn (also formerly a member of the *Bundestag*), like his predecessors in the office of Minister-President of North Rhine-Westphalia, has great influence in the national leadership of his party, and was involved in the coalition-building talks of 1969, for instance. It is, indeed, the very opportunity for exercising political, as well as administrative, leadership that makes this office, or the chance of it (for, like Köppler (CDU) in North Rhine-Westphalia in 1970 and Dröscher (SPD) in Rhineland-Pfalz in 1971, a Bonn-based challenger is not always successful!), preferable to membership of the *Bundestag* or appointment to any but the most influential of the ministries in the Federal Government.

One position of political leadership which is lacking in the Federal Republic (as it is also in the United States) is that of leader of the opposition. This does not automatically revert to the defeated Chancellor-candidate, nor does it go automatically to the leader of the major opposition party. Thus neither Brandt, after his defeats in the campaigns of 1961 and 1965, nor Kiesinger after 1969 came to be regarded as *the* leader of the opposition. If this position can be said to be in the process of emerging, it is becoming associated with the leadership of the opposition *Fraktion*, which accounted for the political strength of Rainer Barzel as challenger for the leadership of the CDU after the 1969 defeat. The lack of such a formal office has favoured the Government of the day, and made the work of the opposition less coherent and less effective.

In the Federal Republic, as in Britain, America and other party-based democracies, party leadership is an important form of political leadership generally. The Federal Chancellor, and the Ministers-President of the *Länder*, are drawn from the party elites, and, secondly, party leaders influence the electoral, organisational and programmatic strategies of their parties in ways which have direct consequences for West German politics.[10] The qualities that might be most appro-

[10] Many examples could be cited, among them Adenauer's relegation of

priate for the formal and public positions of political leadership are not necessarily those that enable a politician to achieve a leading role within his political party. The negative may be true: a Chancellor who is not successful in controlling his party, for instance, may be forced, as in Erhard's case, to make way for someone else. Another consequence of the distinction between public and party leadership is the existence of powerful political leaders who do not simultaneously hold any prominent public office: the leaders of the *Fraktion* organisations, the party general secretaries, and certain local 'bosses', for instance. Men like Herbert Wehner (the leader of the SPD *Fraktion*), Bruno Heck (CDU general secretary), Wolfgang Mischnick (FDP *Fraktion* leader) and Hans-Jürgen Wischniewski (SPD general secretary) are powerful within their political parties, but do not hold public offices commensurate with this importance.

In view of the policy of deliberate selectivity of the occupation powers after the war, the political leaders since 1945 have generally shared certain characteristics which may not hold so strongly in the future. Brandt, Ollenhauer, Schumacher and, to a lesser extent, Adenauer had all suffered directly at the hands of the Nazis. Apart from Adenauer, few of the leading politicians after 1949 have possessed much pre-war leadership experience at national, *Land* or city level. All have been long-serving politicians before reaching leadership positions, with the exception of Erhard, and even he served many years in the shadow of Adenauer, and had filled important executive positions at *Land* and zonal levels after the war before entering the Cabinet.

The party chairmen – and thus usually the Chancellor-candidates for the next election[11] – are selected by the party conference, though only after processes of informal consultation, lobbying and discussion at various levels inside the party. Indeed, in some ways there is a process of 'emergence' similar to that in the British Conservative Party. Brandt, for

---

unification to lesser priority in the CDU programme in the 1949–53 period, Schumacher's embracement of the strategy of opposition rather than collaboration after 1949, the FDP 'Düsseldorf revolt' in 1956, and their 'new course' under Scheel after 1968.

[11] It should be noted that Erhard had to wait nearly three years after becoming Chancellor, before Adenauer resigned the party chairmanship.

instance, was chosen to succeed Ollenhauer, after the elections of 1953 and 1957 had failed to produce the successes the party had hoped for, and in order to give the post-Godesberg image of the SPD a new figure as leader. Kiesinger was elected Chancellor-candidate in 1966 by the CDU–CSU *Fraktion*, against the rival candidacies of Gerstenmaier, Schröder and Barzel, since the resignation of Erhard took place between elections.[12] At the CDU congress in May 1967, Kiesinger was elected party chairman.

A major problem with political leaders is their multiplicity of function. They must make decisions and determine policy, for the nation and within the party; they must exercise authority, but must conciliate when necessary; they must keep conflict within limits, yet prevent the spread of apathy; they must represent the Government of the day and its broad ideals, yet promote the interests and policies of the party they lead. The very incompatibility of some of these tasks imposes strains on even the best leaders. For the less-than-best, they can be frustrating, and make the task of leadership impossible.

POLITICAL ELITES

Elites are minorities who exercise a preponderant influence within a society. Where this influence is exercised on political matters, these minorities may be termed political elites. The identification of such elites is no easy task. As with political leadership, political influence does not coincide at all exactly with the occupation of formal positions in politics. Indeed, groups outside the formal political structure – in the economic system, in the Army or the churches, for instance – may have to be included as members of the political elite because of their undeniable influence on political outcomes. In the Federal Republic, the political elite includes members of the Government, members of the *Bundestag* and *Bundesrat*, leading civil servants, the top-level members of the party bureaucracies, leading *Land* politicians and party officials, certain highly influential members of the Press and the radio and television services, a number of professors, members of the economic and other advisory committees, several influential

[12] On the third ballot, Kiesinger got 137 votes, Schröder 81 and Barzel 26. Gerstenmaier dropped out before the third ballot.

churchmen, and a number of the leading members of the armed services, industry, the diplomatic service, the law, and interest-groups such as the trade unions, agriculture and the commercial world. Even this list would not be complete.

Several studies have been made of the social characteristics of members of the West German elite. Wolfgang Zapf[13] found that, not unexpectedly, they are mostly members of the upper or upper-middle class, and that, depending on which part of the elite is examined, between 50 per cent and 100 per cent had university education, many of them in law. On average, they were in their early fifties, and very few were younger than forty years old. For the most part, the elite has been male and Protestant. Both Scheuch[14] and Dahrendorf[15] have emphasised the lack of a common 'life-style' among members of the elite; it is not meaningful, in the West German context, to speak of an 'establishment' or a ruling class because members of the elite share little in the way of common background – they do not form a single stratum of society, they do not share a similar educational or occupational history – or contemporary interests; even their mutual contact is limited much more to 'business' than in the case of Britain or the United States. Once again, however, few of these characteristics are much different from those to be found increasingly in other industrialised societies. The growing political influence of managerial elites from commerce and industry, the increase of administrative influence on decision-making, the increase in opportunities for entry into elite positions for members of the middle classes in particular, the decline in influence of the military and the aristocracy – these are factors which, it is true, differentiate contemporary German elites from their pre-Hitler predecessors, but they are also the aspects of West German elites which display the greatest similarity to elites in other industrialised societies.

Political elites are important not only for the influence they might exercise on political decisions but also because they serve as a reservoir of potential political leaders. It is difficult

[13] W. Zapf, 'Führungsgruppen in West- und Ost-Deutschland', in W. Zapf (ed.), *Beiträge zur Analyse der deutschen Oberschicht* (Munich, 2nd ed., 1965).

[14] E. Scheuch, 'Sichtbare und unsichtbare Macht' and 'Die Macht hat viele Herren', *Die Zeit*, 24 Nov. and 11 Dec. 1967.

[15] Dahrendorf, *Society and Democracy in Germany*, chap. 17.

to envisage a situation where a President, Chancellor or Minister-President was appointed without having been a long-serving member of the political elite. They also act as intermediaries between the political authorities and the public, either generally (e.g. as members of the *Bundestag* or as leading civil servants) or as representatives of interest-groups (leading industrialists, church leaders, trade union officials). Thus, though perhaps not *representative* of all sections of West German society, the political elite as a whole may be judged so far to have been fairly *responsive* to demands and pressures on the political system.

The recruitment of political elites takes place in a variety of ways. The German tradition of paternalistic 'adoption' by a superior, who then acts as mentor, can still be influential in shaping the careers of academics, business executives, bureaucrats and politicians. Success in one field can be used as a means of entry into another, so businessmen such as Rosenthal and Pieroth enter politics, while politicians such as Mende are able to obtain high-ranking commercial appointments.[16] Of all the routes of entry into the political elite, the most significant is election to the *Bundestag*, since political leaders are generally drawn from the ranks of the legislature.

Selection as a party candidate for the *Bundestag* can take one of two forms. For constituency candidates, selection is in the hands of the constituency party. The main advantage here is to be the sitting member, or, if the seat is held by the opposition, to have 'nursed' the constituency as a list-elected member. Renomination, while not as automatic as in Britain, is rarely withheld without good cause – though challenges to such renomination, e.g. by members of the party's youth movement, are becoming increasingly frequent. Religion is sometimes taken into account, Catholic candidates being preferred for predominantly Catholic areas, Protestants for Protestant areas, especially in the CDU. Local residence, occupation, political experience (e.g. in *Land* or local government) and age are also relevant factors. Women find it difficult to gain nomination for constituency seats, and the greater proportion of those elected are elected from *Land* lists. For the

[16] Rosenthal (SPD) is a director of the famous porcelain firm; Pieroth (CDU) a director of a wine merchant and producer firm; Mende (FDP) became a member of IOS. See also 'Manager nach Bonn', *Capital*, Apr. 1971.

Länder lists, selection is by some form of *Land* delegate conference, with a proposed list presented by the *Land* party executive, which is then open to modification by the conference. Considerations of importance here are the sharing of seats among the autonomous regional organisations of the party (where a *Land* contains more than one such organisation), religious proportionality, the inclusion of a representative of the women's and youth organisations of the party in the 'safe' places near the top of the list, and a broad representation of occupations and interests. The selection of these lists can often lead to a power struggle in the party. The younger, and more left-wing, members of the FDP in North Rhine-Westphalia in 1969, for instance, demonstrated considerable strength (though generally unsuccessfully) in trying to modify the composition of the *Land* list.[17]

While certain trends are observable in the characteristics of the West German political elite – its heterogeneous nature, the pressures of the younger generation for political influence, the broadening of the social-class base of elite recruitment – it is still too early to make firm statements about the types of elites that are likely to be most consonant with the post-war political culture and the political institutions of the Bonn regime. Only now is the first post-war generation of the political elite beginning to emerge. After 1945, the situation was so fluid, so indeterminate, that not only leaders such as Adenauer and Schumacher could define their own roles reasonably freely but the second-rank members of the elite, the trade union hierarchies, leading industrialists interested in politics, members of the *Bundestag*, leading civil servants, were also relatively unrestrained by any cultural expectations of their roles. Edinger's statement about Schumacher is still, to some extent, valid about today's elites: 'Surviving elements of past German political cultures and sub-cultures, as well as the authority of the occupation powers, set limits upon what an aspiring leader could do. But to a large extent political conditions and roles were comparatively unstructured, particularly in the first years, waiting to be moulded into more

[17] For further information on candidate selection, see Kitzinger, *German Electoral Politics*, chap. iv, 'The Selection of Candidates'; Loewenberg, *Parliament in the German Political System*, pp. 67–84; *Der Spiegel*, 7 July 1969, pp. 32–45: 'Die Vatermörder'.

stable patterns by the interaction of leading players, German and non-German.'[18] A more structured set of elite roles may now be emerging, particularly as a result of the transfer of power from the CDU to the SPD and the entry into politics of the post-war generation. Such a development would be beneficial to the survival, and the stability, of democratic politics in West Germany.

[18] Edinger, *Kurt Schumacher*, p. 310.

PART FOUR

Political Issues

11 West German Politics Today

THE POLITICAL SITUATION

The 1969 election campaign commenced very early indeed. It could be said to have begun with the formation of the Grand Coalition in 1966. Certainly the knowledge that this coalition might come to an end as a result of the 1969 elections, that all parties had much to gain but also much at risk in that election, overshadowed political events in 1968. This gave rise to problems within the coalition, for both partners were anxious to be associated with the successes of the Government, but to implicate the other party in any failures and difficulties. The FDP began more strongly to seek a distinctive profile as a 'third force' rather than the reluctant, but fairly reliable, liberalising partner of the CDU. Its new leader, Scheel, and the influence of its young and active radical supporters were major factors in this development. By January 1969 it was publicising its new stance, in an effort to win early – and, perhaps, lasting – attention from the electorate. In March, for the first time since 1949, the election of a new President of the Federal Republic occurred in the same year as the *Bundestag* elections. The two candidates were Schröder (CDU) and Heinemann (SPD). The decision of the majority of the FDP to vote for Heinemann not only gave him victory on the third ballot but served notice that the party was now very ready to consider entering a coalition headed by the SPD, and could no longer automatically be considered as supporters of the CDU in government. Thus no result was impossible in terms of Government formation, if the FDP overcame the 5 per cent limitation. The CDU and, though hardly with much probability, the SPD, might be able to govern alone. Either party could hope to construct a coalition with the FDP. Or the Grand Coalition could continue, as many voters and not a few of the prominent figures of each party in the existing Government hoped. The unknown factor in the calculations – apart from the relative party strengths – was the NPD. Though early opinion polls showed that it was unlikely that they would surmount the 5 per cent hurdle, nevertheless the *Landtag* victories in Bremen, Hesse and Bavaria, the fears that they would conduct a very aggressive campaign, doubts about the effects on the voters of student demonstrations, the permissive society, law and order as an issue, and the new *Ostpolitik* pursued by Brandt as Foreign Minister all raised questions about the reliability of such forecasts as predictions of the National Democratic Party's eventual vote in September.

The campaign itself was vigorous. The CDU campaign emphasised the experience of the party in governing, and the need for continuity. Its programme, entitled 'Secure in the Seventies', while emphasising its awareness of the need for progress, tried to distinguish its own experience and pragmatism from the 'illusions' of the SPD. In foreign policy, the party promised a willingness to negotiate with the countries of East Europe only if there were signs of genuine response, but strongly stressed West Germany's attachment to a united Europe and the Western Alliance. Other recurrent themes were the rejection of radicalism of the left or of the right, and the function of the election as a clear choice between Kiesinger and Brandt (the results of opinion polls on this point had reinforced the party's natural tendency to build its strategy around the Chancellor himself, and to focus attention on him). The SPD stressed their contribution to the policies of the Grand Coalition, and, whereas the CDU had presented an 'electoral' programme (*Wahlprogramm*), the SPD confidently offered a 'government' programme (*Regierungsprogramm*). They emphasised the talents of their team and one of their major themes was a series of posters consisting of photographs of prominent leaders, Brandt, Schiller, Helmut Schmidt, Kuhn, Wehner, Ehmke and others, under various slogans concerning party policies or strategies. Also stressed were Brandt's foreign visits as a member of the Grand Coalition, and the wide range of types of people who were SPD voters, underlining its claim to be a 'people's party' rather than a class party. Their main attack on the CDU related to the failure to control the monetary situation, and it was well known that Schiller had long favoured a revaluation of the

Deutschmark, but that this had been blocked by the CDU and CSU members of the Cabinet. Their policy orientation was that of new directions for a new decade, in foreign policy (especially towards West Germany's Communist neighbours), education, social and economic policy, summed up in their slogan 'We create the modern Germany'. The FDP campaign was intended to differentiate the party clearly from their rivals, and from its own past image as a 'trimming' centre party which generally supported the CDU. The first phase of its campaign was aimed at radical reform of what it regarded as outdated attitudes: to the Eastern bloc, the school system, the federal structure, the Grand Coalition itself. Then came more specific policies, based on the 'Concept of the FDP' entitled 'Practical Policies for Germany' endorsed by the Nürnberg party congress in June 1969. The tone of the party's publicity was that of responsibility, of seriousness. A readiness to consider a coalition with the SPD was emphasised from the beginning. The NPD campaign was defensive, in that they sought to show that they were not a violent party of extremits, and they had hanging over them the very real threat of a challenge to their constitutionality in the Federal Constitutional Court. Demonstrations against them, and the publicity given to their own counter-measures (carefully screened audiences being admitted only on payment of an entry fee, political meetings patrolled by tough-looking stewards), ensured that their campaign would not be allowed to proceed quietly. The campaigns of the minor parties, such as the ADF (*Aktion Demokratische Fortschritt*) and the *Europa Partei*, though confined to only a few areas, added a colourful irrelevance to the scene.

During the campaign, several political events became incorporated as issues into the party battle, such as foreign affairs, the currency problems, demonstrations, and, in September, a series of 'wildcat strikes'. But the effect of these was diffuse. The strikes probably came too late to do much harm, or confer much benefit, for any party, and the quarrel between the CDU and Schiller over revaluation never seemed to rise very far above the technicalities of monetary economics. In the end, it was the broad party images held by the voters that mattered most, rather than any particular issues.

The result of the election did not at first give indication of which Government would be formed of the remaining possibilities: a continuation of the Grand Coalition, or a coalition of the FDP with one or other of the major parties. CDU leaders on election night were clearly optimistic, in view of their retention of the status of largest party in the *Bundestag*. But the attitude of the FDP was rapidly made clear: subject to negotiations, they would hope to form a coalition with the SPD. Telephone calls between Brandt and Scheel were made even as the results continued to come in, and talks began on 30 September. The coalition negotiations took place over a period of seventeen days, the shortest formation period of any Government in the Federal Republic's history.[1] Despite statements made by the CDU leadership of readiness to discuss terms with the FDP, and strong reservations from Erich Mende, the former leader of the FDP, and some of his conservative colleagues about their support for a left-wing coalition, an announcement was made on 3 October 1969 that the SPD and FDP had reached agreement on the formation of a coalition. The FDP secured three posts in the new Government: the Foreign and Interior ministries, and Agriculture, as well as a generous share of second-rank posts. The expected working majority of the new Government was small (only twelve seats), but, unless there were large-scale defections from the disgruntled conservatives in the FDP, it would be enough for most purposes.

The consequences of the post-election situation for the parties were varied indeed. For the SPD the opportunities were considerable. Their pragmatic, reforming image seemed to be winning new types of voter, particularly young voters and voters in the cities. If the FDP should disappear, the SPD could expect the balance of the benefit. There would be substantial advantages to be obtained from having the Chancellor as their party leader, and the authority – and the publicity – of being the Government. If, in addition, some of their reforms of, for instance, social policy, education or foreign relations were successful, their record in 1973 would be almost impervious to opposition criticism. For the FDP, the danger signals were clear. The party could no longer hope to retreat, to win back its old national-liberal voters. Therefore it had to

[1] U. Bermbach, 'Stationen der Regierungsbildung 1969', *Zeitschrift für Parlamentsfragen*, 1 1 (June 1970) 23.

make its profile as a non-socialist reforming party more unambiguous, and it had to combine co-operation with the SPD in the Government with a distinction of policy stance in the eyes of the electorate. It would be able to use the *Land* elections as trial runs for 1973, but the continued existence of the party was clearly at stake. The CDU and CSU now had to learn the skills of opposition. This offered the opportunity to rethink their policies, and to formulate a fresh programme, probably under a younger leader, at the next federal election. They remained the largest of the parties, and could hope for an absolute majority in 1973 should the new Government's policies fail to secure support. But they would lack the prestige of having the Chancellor to lead them (and in the words of their own 1969 slogan 'It all depends on the Chancellor'). And the *Land* elections, while providing platforms for a continuing attack on the Government, would mean that they could not be used by the CDU for a complete renunciation of the past, in terms of policies or leaders. The NPD faced four problems. The election result had not given them their hoped-for representation in Bonn; the formation of a new Government had switched publicity from the NPD to the coalition; the campaign had cost money and had left the party with heavy debts to pay off; and the party had, if anything, more of a reputation for violent tactics and radical policies than before the election.[2] The extreme left gained nothing from the election. Its front party, the ADF, won only a handful of votes, and there seemed to be no favourable auguries for the future. The new Government would not be less firm than the old when it came to demonstrations and political violence of the left wing or the right wing, while the failure of the NPD removed a major excuse for such activities on the part of the 'extra-parliamentary opposition'.

The replacement of the Grand Coalition by the new SPD–FDP coalition came to be referred to as a 'change of power' (*Machtwechsel*). While this might be somewhat of an exaggeration, in view of the importance of the role of the SPD in the Grand Coalition,[3] a significant change had occurred in

[2] The trial of a former NPD member for the shooting of two demonstrators in Kassel during the election campaign did the party no service.

[3] W. Kaltefleiter *et al.*, 'Im Wechselspiel der Koalitionen', a special issue of *Verfassung und Verfassungswirklichkeit* (Köln, 1970) pp. 9–13.

that the Chancellorship, for the first time since the war, was no longer filled by a Christian Democrat, and, also for the first time, the CDU–CSU were in opposition. These were welcome indications that, after twenty years of dominance by the CDU, the system could allow and accommodate a change of this type.[4] Given the prospect that the FDP might fail to win 5 per cent of the vote in 1973, and given the fact that the SPD won more of the directly elected seats than the CDU–CSU, the result also increased the possibility of a two-party *Bundestag*, possibly elected by a British non-proportional style of franchise, in the near future, with a more regular alternation of the parties in power.

Brandt's Cabinet-building proceeded fairly smoothly. Besides the Chancellor and the three FDP ministers, the SPD members of the previous Government and the party 'prominents' were included: Helmut Schmidt (Defence), Karl Schiller (Economics), Alex Möller (Finance) and Horst Ehmke (Chancellor's Department). Herbert Wehner became leader of the parliamentary party. *Land* and trade union interests were taken into account, and one non-party expert, Leussink (Education and Scientific Research), was included.[5] The size of the Cabinet was reduced by four seats, owing to the elimination of the ministries of Posts (amalgamated with Transport), Family Affairs, Refugees and the Treasury, whose functions were redistributed among other departments. Along with other political changes (see above, Chapter 8) the impression was given of a well-prepared programme of structural alteration, ready for the introduction of a series of substantive reforms, both of internal and external policies, as forecast in the Government Declaration of 28 October 1969, to be amplified in a series of policy statements on the state of the nation, the economy, agriculture, education, defence, transport, health, urban planning, tax reform and other matters, which, it was promised, would be published in the first year or so of the new Government's existence.

The CDU–CSU had to adapt to its new role of opposition. As an opposition, it could call on many talented leaders: Bar-

[4] Brandt, in the 1969 Government Declaration, spoke of the West German parliamentary democracy as having exhibited its ability to permit change, and thus that it had 'passed its test'.

[5] For the full Cabinet (as at July 1971), see Appendix B below.

zel, the leader of the parliamentary party, Strauss, the CSU leader, Schröder, the defeated presidential candidate, Kiesinger, Katzer, the influential leader of the CDU's social committee, and many others. The party also had the opportunity of making the role of opposition more effective and more acceptable within the political system. The SPD had been, in some ways, a 'natural' opposition, not completely free in people's minds from notions of opposition to the state as well as to the Government, partly because of the linkages between 'socialism' and the Communist states to the east, for instance. The new opposition could never be accused of lacking in patriotism, acceptance of the constitution, or of connections, however tenuous, with the Communists. But, despite promises of co-operation by the CDU,[6] the early impression given by the CDU–CSU was that of negativism. In part, this was due to the need for time to adjust to an unfamiliar role. In part also, it arose from doubts about its future leadership. In part it was encouraged by the emphasis which the Government placed in their first year of office on the *Ostpolitik*, and which the CDU could quite credibly denounce without the necessity of suggesting a constructive alternative. With the settlement of its leadership problem,[7] this negativism can be expected to be considerably reduced and modified. The new leader will have to present a more distinctive set of policy alternatives, and greater concentration by the Brandt Government on internal policies will also have this effect on the opposition. The *Land* elections in 1970–1 have also required the opposition to state its national policies more positively in order to win votes.

During the first two years of the new Government, *Land* elections have taken place in Hamburg, North Rhine-Westphalia, Lower Saxony, Saarland, Hesse, Bavaria, West Berlin, Rhineland-Pfalz, Schleswig-Holstein and Bremen. These elections were fought very much on the basis of the new Federal Government's record. The propaganda of the parties, the numerous visits by leading politicians from all parties in the

[6] Barzel's reply to the Government Declaration of 28 October 1969 contained a specific reference to the offer of co-operation on 'vital questions of the nation' by his party (*Die Welt*, 30 Oct. 1969).

[7] In October 1971 Barzel was elected chairman of the CDU by the party conference.

Bundestag, the attention given by the media to the campaigns and the results, all demonstrate this. As an example, during a meeting in Köln on 2 June 1970 as part of the North Rhine-Westphalia election campaign, Rainer Barzel, the CDU *Fraktion* leader, concentrated in his speech entirely on issues of national policy: the three themes of the educational policy of the SPD, inflation and rising prices, and foreign policy. The questions he dealt with after this speech were similarly centred on such themes and on the CDU's own policies in opposition. In terms of the verdicts of these elections on the new coalition, the CDU, aided by the return of former NPD voters to the party, clearly more than held its own *vis-à-vis* the 1969 federal election results. On the other hand, the SPD rarely lost more than a percentage point, so they also had no cause for pessimism. The FDP did badly until the Hesse vote (where probably they were helped by a temporary 'loan' of voters from the SPD), and returned to the Bavarian *Landtag* after an absence of four years, though in June they had lost their representation in the Saarland and Lower Saxony parliaments.[8]

ECONOMIC POLICIES AND PROBLEMS

The West German economy has passed through several phases since 1945. First hampered, then stimulated, by the enormous tasks of reconstruction, the combination of the currency reform, American aid, the stimulation to trade caused by the Korean war, and Erhard's social-market economics produced the 'economic miracle' of the 1950s. The establishment of the European Economic Community led to a period of consolidation during which the Federal Republic became the dominant European economy, and, in many respects, second only to the United States. The economic crisis of 1965 was overcome, and recovery took place under the Grand Coalition, despite differences in policy between Schiller, the Economics Minister, and Strauss, the Finance Minister. But before the new SPD–FDP coalition came to power in 1969 it had become evident that this recovery was accompanied by clear indications of inflation.

One measure of adjustment which Schiller had pressed for several times during 1969 in the period before the elections

[8] For *Land* election results, see Appendix D below.

was a revaluation of the *Deutschmark*. Strauss, supported by his Cabinet colleagues from the CDU, refused to agree, and the matter became a major election issue. The continuation of inflation, and speculative currency inflows during the later stages of the campaign as it became clear that an SPD-led Government could be formed, made action by Schiller after the election inevitable. Though the FDP members of the Cabinet, with an eye to their electoral support, would not agree to the proposed upward change of over 10 per cent which Schiller wanted, a revaluation of 8·5 per cent took place on 27 October 1969.

The situation improved but little. In March 1970 the West German bank rate was raised to a record post-war level of 7·5 per cent. Federal, *Land* and local authority expenditures were postponed or reduced. Fiscal and monetary restrictions were imposed, and attempts made to encourage savings and limit price increases. In July a repayable tax surcharge of 10 per cent was introduced on income and corporation taxes, and reductions were made in investment allowances. Attempts to co-ordinate the efforts of the Government, the unions and business undertakings, under the title of *Konzertierten Aktion* (concerted action), a group which met from time to time to discuss, e.g., wage–price guidelines, were not apparently very successful. By the middle of 1971 the problem remained the same: wages chased prices, capital flowed into the country from abroad, and there were further rumours of another revaluation. The choice before the Government concerning economic policy is not an easy one. On the one hand, harsh restrictive policies, leading to further strikes over refused wage claims, increases in unemployment, stagnation of the economy and the abandonment of the costly programmes of internal reform which the Government has in view, would lead to a potentially explosive political situation. The alternative, of allowing an annual rate of inflation of about 5 per cent, introducing proposed reforms but at increasing levels of Government expenditure, is almost equally unacceptable to a nation whose economy depends on maintaining a competitive trading position. In either case, the Government's intention of avoiding substantial tax increases would have to be abandoned. But again, the influence of Germany's own past is powerful: memories of the hyper-inflation of 1922–3 linger, and make more imperative control of the rate of price increases.

TABLE 10

The 1969 Budget (83,346 million DM)

Income	%	*Expenditure*	%
Turnover tax	38·7	Social services	27·9
Customs duty and consumer tax	26·9	Defence	23·2
		Economic assistance	11·4
Income and corporation tax	23·0	Transport and communication	11·2
Miscellaneous	11·4	Governmental services	4·7
		Other items	21·6

Source: Government Annual Report, 1970.

TABLE 11

Cost-of-living Index (1962 = 100)

1963	*1964*	*1965*	*1966*	*1967*	*1968*	*1969*	*1970*
103	105	109	113	114	116	120	126

Source: Monthly Report of the *Deutsche Bundesbank*, Feb. 1971.

Associated particularly with economic policy, but a fundamental aspect of many other policy areas, are the taxation and budgetary policies of the Federal Government. The development of a medium-term financial plan to cover the remainder of the legislative period to mid-1973 was promised in the Government Declaration of October 1969. This plan, and the work of the Financial Planning Advisory Council (*Finanzplanungsrat*) to recommend measures for the better co-ordination of the budgetary policies and financial plans of the federal, *Land* and local authorities, will permit a more efficient co-ordination of policy proposals and the financial resources necessary for their implementation. Various taxation reforms are under consideration, in keeping with the Brandt Government's promise of a just and efficient taxation system, and consideration has been given, for instance, to the closing of tax loopholes for residents who have property or income abroad. An independent committee of experts was appointed by Strauss (the then Minister of Finance) in 1968 to examine taxation reforms, and reported in April 1971. However, its proposals tended to be in the direction of increasing the already relatively high bias in the West German system in favour of indirect, rather than direct, taxation (a bias shared by other EEC countries, and far greater than in the United States or Britain). The SPD coalition requires a growing amount of governmental income for its reforms, but party pressures in the SPD will not be willing to accept an increase in the taxation of the working man's pay-packet as the method of finding such extra finance.

A major interest of the Social Democrats for some time has been the furtherance of worker participation in decision-making within the firm. In particular, this policy of co-determination was one of the major issues during the 1969 election, and on taking office Brandt promised close examination of the report of the Biedenkopf Commission on 'Co-determination within the Firm', set up in January 1968. This committee presented its recommendations in January 1970. It defined co-determination as the institutionalised participation of the employee or his representative in the decision process of the firm, and concluded by suggesting that the existing law, which, outside the coal and steel industries, gave only one-third of the seats on the works council to employees, be changed to give employees a ratio of five seats to the employers' seven, one of each delegation to be a co-opted member. This proposal disappointed some left-wing socialists and trade unionists, who had hoped that the commission would recommend parity, five members from each side and an independent chairman. These proposals were embodied in a bill in October 1970, put forward by the Government after taking account of the representations of the other coalition partner, the FDP, and the opinions of employers' and workers' organisations. A major concern of the CDU, who do not go on record as opposing co-determination in principle, is the extent to which workers' representatives in the 26,000 or so works councils affected by the law will be drawn from full-time trade union officials, external to the firms on whose councils they will sit.

Another change made by the present Government in favour of employees was a doubling of the upper limits of the savings and investment scheme, subsidised by the Government, under which employees can contract to invest a fixed monthly sum deducted from their wages, subject to certain conditions about withdrawal. This is designed to encourage wage-earners to build up a capital sum, both for reasons of social justice and, as a consequent effect, increasing the amount of money available for investment rather than consumption in a period of inflation.

Industrial concentration has been an important factor in German economic policy since the cartels of the late nineteenth century. The political influence of large-scale industry during the inter-war years, and the role of Krupp, Thyssen and other industrialists in helping Hitler to power, led to post-war policies of breaking up large firms into smaller units. Despite this, the pressures of the economy have led to a degree of industrial concentration in publishing, banking, automobile production, the chemical industry and many other sectors that has caused successive Governments considerable concern. Legislation was passed in 1957 setting up a Federal Cartel Office to administer the restrictive provisions introduced by the Government, but concessions by the CDU to industrial pressures weakened the force of this legislation. A further law was passed in 1965, strengthening the degree of public control. The Federal Cartel Office reviews industrial take-overs and cartel agreements, and may take legal action against firms which they consider to be in breach of the law against the reduction of competition.

The structure of the industry is also one of the major problems of agricultural policy. As in many other industrialised societies, the legacy of a large number of small farms, operating at little above subsistence level, is not only an economic problem but a social problem as well. Part of this structural problem was caused by the breaking-up of large farms after the war, as part of the land-reform policy and the resettlement of refugees. The Common Market agricultural policy has had the effect, through guaranteed prices, of producing large surpluses of many products, especially butter and milk, which have to be stored, destroyed, given away or sold at low prices to countries outside the European Economic Community. The burden on the taxpayer increases steadily, and despite counter-measures the system encourages small farmers to stay in farming and to produce whatever they can. The new Minister of Agriculture, Ertl (FDP), has forecast that, in line with developments in Common Market policies, the number of farmers will be drastically reduced in West Germany by the middle of the next decade, and that those who do remain will have larger holdings, and be aided by subventions and guaranteed prices to attain a higher standard of living.[9] Whether this can be achieved is doubtful. The costs would be high, higher perhaps than a policy of creating locally alternative employment for small farmers, who could retain their holdings for low-level production on a part-time basis (as, indeed, do many small farmers already). Also, there are well over two million people employed in farming, an influential force when it comes to polling day, especially in Bavaria, Lower Saxony and Schleswig-Holstein. Though the German Farmers' Association is mainly representative of the larger farmers, they too might be opposed to any too-radical changes in the structure of the industry. But meanwhile rising prices for foodstuffs under the controls of the present policies add to inflationary pressures; the farming community is disgruntled at its low standard of living compared to industrial workers in the towns; production increases at about 3 per cent annually, but demand cannot keep up with this increase; any further revaluation of the currency might, as in 1969, require that the farmer be compensated by large state subsidies. Thus agriculture remains a major economic and social problem in West German politics.

SOCIAL POLICIES

'Education and training, science and research stand at the head of those reforms which it is appropriate for us to undertake.'[10] Education has become an area of policy which has commanded increasing attention from the Government in West Germany, and has always had considerable priority in the SPD's electoral publicity. Brandt's appointment of a non-party academic, Leussink, to the Department of Education and Scientific Research in 1969 was an indication that reforms in education would not be based simply on ideological motives. The chief issues of educational policy at all levels are the organisational structure, the financing and the control of schools, colleges and universities, and the provision of oppor-

[9] 'Erbhof 70', *Der Spiegel*, 7 Dec. 1970, pp. 89–90.
[10] Government Declaration of 28 Oct. 1969.

tunities for personal educational development. In particular, the lack of co-ordination among the various types of educational institution, the previously minimal co-operation between the Federal Government and the *Länder*, as paymaster and controllers of education respectively, and the absence of any long-term plan or budget for education, have hampered development in the Federal Republic. It is in the educational sphere that the challenge of East Germany is strongest in relation to the standards of the Federal Republic.

The new coalition took a number of steps towards changing this situation during its first two years of existence. Brandt, in his Government Declaration, pointed to the need for a fifteen- to twenty-year long-term plan for education, and a national education budget on a five- to fifteen-year basis. In January 1970 a planning committee on university education was created, consisting of Leussink and Möller (the Minister of Finance) and eleven *Land* representatives. This was based on Article 91(*b*) of the Basic Law, added to the constitution in May 1969, permitting co-operation between the Federation and the *Länder* on educational planning and scientific research. In June 1970 an agreement was signed which set up a joint Federation–*Länder* commission for educational planning, which first met in July of that year, and which was to produce recommendations for the integrated planning of education, both in the form of a long-term outline plan and short-term implementation plans. In addition, the Education Council (*Bildungsrat*) and the Science Council (*Wissenschaftsrat*) also have competence for aspects of educational planning. The priorities given to educational expansion require that the proportion of the gross national product devoted to education and research must double by 1980.

Many reform proposals have also been made in the area of pre-university education, though in many cases it is difficult to achieve general agreement on the content of such reforms, and many groups with vested interests in the *status quo* would obstruct any changes proposed. The question of the church schools and of religious instruction in schools is raised at every election. As a result of the freedom of parents to have schools of their choice, many very small villages or rural regions have a Catholic, a Protestant and a non-denominational school, each with only a handful of pupils of diverse ages, and a small number of staff. To counter this at the secondary level, and to overcome the inflexibility of the system of differential secondary schools (the approximate equivalents of secondary modern, secondary technical and grammar schools in Britain), a form of comprehensive secondary school (the *Gesamtschule*) has been introduced in some *Länder* such as Hamburg, Hesse and North Rhine-Westphalia. Other changes are pressed for in the training of teachers, the curricula and the school-leaving and school-starting ages.

At the level of higher education, the problems are those common to many other countries, exacerbated by the particularly rigid traditions of German university life: democratisation by student participation in decision-making, more places in those faculties where the *numerus clausus* (limited intake) operates, a move towards the integration of various forms of higher education institution (the *Gesamthochschule*), more grants for students from low-income families, alteration in the status of the non-professorial teaching staff (the *Assistenten*), and more co-ordination of university planning on a national basis. Opposition to the extension of student co-determination into the areas of course content and research, the traditional preserves of the professor, has been particularly marked, and this opposition resulted in the founding of a society, the *Bund Freiheit der Wissenschaft,* in Bad Godesberg in October 1970, for the protection of scientific freedom, led by a number of prominent professors and politicians.

The SPD has always given considerable attention to social security policies, and it is therefore no surprise to find in their electoral publicity and in the Government Declaration a number of statements promising reform and improvement of the 'welfare state' aspects of government policy. After the war, even under the CDU-led Governments from 1949 onwards, the comprehensive nature of West Germany's social security system was marked, building as it did on a tradition reaching back to Bismarck. The CDU itself was prompted by its own 'social committee', and by the need not to be 'outbid' in election campaigns by the SPD. However, it has also had to listen to its supporters from industry and from the higher income groups, who wish to limit the burden of contributions to social security funds which they have to pay. The system has not always been equitable; it has not always kept pace with economic and social changes; it has not always provided assistance to those most in need of it. The Brandt Government has introduced a revised system of health insurance, of a more comprehensive nature. Hospital building is high on its list of priorities. Family allowance payments have been increased. Attention has been given to the improvement of industrial injury compensation and sick-pay rates, along with other measures under the general heading of 'security in the workplace'. A revision and broadening of the state old-age pension scheme was also forecast in the Government Declaration.

After education and social security, the general realm of environmental policy has received priority. Under this heading are included not only the newly fashionable concerns with pollution, noise, ecology and conservation but also the more traditional problems of transportation, environmental planning and housing. These are, of course, all intimately related, and any policies concerned with their reform must be closely co-ordinated if their effects are not to be disadvantageous: the siting of new factories, housing estates and autobahns, the control of river pollution, the provision of cheap and efficient public transport in an increasingly mobile society, the problems of controlling the car and the juggernaut freight-lorries. The scattering of these responsibilities over the ministries of the Interior (conservation and anti-pollution policies), Transport, Posts and Communications, and Housing and Town Planning does not make the problems of co-ordination easier to solve.

Brandt has frequently emphasised[11] that his Government was giving environmental protection policies a priority position in social policy. He has promised that a comprehensive programme for immediate action will be presented to the *Bundestag*. Such a programme would require not only international co-operation if it were to be effective but also more power being transferred to the Federal Government rather than environmental policy remaining as a concurrent responsibility of the Federation and the *Länder*. To this end, a constitutional amendment was proposed by the Minister of the Interior, Genscher, in the *Bundestag* in December 1970

[11] For example at a meeting in connection with the European Nature Conservancy Year in Bonn (*Die Welt*, 30 Nov. 1970) and in the 1969 Government Declaration.

which gave rise to a debate on the broad subject of environmental protection.[12] In particular, clean air, pure water and a reduction in noise were mentioned as urgent matters for Government attention. A court case involving the dumping of industrial wastes in the Rhine at the end of 1970 also gave publicity to the problem of pollution. However, policies, to be effective, would cost considerable sums of money, and though there seems to be all-party agreement on the desirability of protecting and improving the environment, it is by no means certain that debates on appropriations or the imposition of high preventative costs on factories, automobile users or air travellers, for example, would be able to avoid pressure from lobbies of those directly affected.

As one of the most devastated of European countries, Germany had to rebuild many of her factories, schools, offices, hospitals and homes after the war was over. Initially, this was done on a replacement basis, but under the new regime after 1949 more attention was given to planning, and to new forms of housing, house-building and financing. The rapid increase in population as refugees moved westward added to the pressure for new housing. Consequently, the construction industry has been of central importance to the economy, and the costs of building materials, of land and of wages in the industry have tended to rise rapidly because of scarcity of supply. Rents and selling prices of flats and houses have also increased, which has led to overcrowding in the cities, to bad living conditions and other problems, as well as to the increase in political activity in many cities on the part of the rent-payer. However, these problems have also stimulated some solutions, including the encouragement of various forms of 'social housing' and publicly owned dwellings.

The building programme and the spread of cities outwards, leading in some cases to the development of conurbations (e.g. in the Ruhr and in the Köln region), have given increased significance to town planning in West Germany. The realisation that sociological as well as physical considerations must be taken into account in such planning has been growing, with the result that some developments in West German cities are taken as models for the rest of Europe. Nor has it been sufficient simply to plan and develop. Transport is a

[12] *Die Welt*, 17 Dec. 1970.

vital element in modern urban life, and West Germany has not escaped the pressures of the motor-car and the relative decline in the usage of public transport. In the cities, where congestion and transport costs are rapidly increasing burdens, various experiments with computerised traffic control and new underground railways and urban motorways have been tried. There is even the suggestion of a zero-charge public transport system being introduced in some cities, in an effort to reduce the costs of congestion. The national railway network is being developed and electrification has reached near-completion. The motorway system is comprehensive, and policies for controlling goods-vehicle usage at weekends and other periods of heavy traffic seem to work well. All these problems of environmental policies are once again illustrative of the extent to which important issues in West German politics, the questions discussed in the Cabinet and in the *Bundestag*, or in political forums at *Land* and local levels, that occupy the time of the Government planners and the major departments, are so very similar to those which other industrialised, urban and mobile societies also find on their agenda of 'unfinished political business'.

West Germany also has its share of miscellaneous social problems which from time to time are given publicity in the tabloid Press or the illustrated magazines: drugs, divorce, pornography, the 'permissive society', the abortion controversy and so on. These tend not to be party-political issues as such, and are once again by no means confined to West German society. But they may be used as evidence by radical groups that there is need for political interference, either on the side of greater freedom, or to provide more control. The *Gastarbeiter* (foreign workers) question is of a similar nature. These workers, mostly from poorer Mediterranean countries, have provided the West German economy with an appreciable part of its labour force in recent years. Yet they are often housed in barrack-type camps, or get poor-quality lodgings, they are prone to difficulties of various kinds because of the language problem, and they are the target of suspicious resentment from their German neighbours. Certainly in a time of depression there could be powerful voices raised to demand their repatriation, and nationalistic groups as it is do not hesitate to blame many of the troubles of West German society on these people. There could even be envisaged political situations arising in the future where these workers themselves become 'politicised' and impose collective demands on the system.

DEFENCE AND SECURITY

Though many of the political issues and problems of economic and social policy are those to be found in most of the industrialised societies of the West – inflation, the mixed economy, educational facilities, the situation in agriculture, transport, the environment – the problems which the Federal Republic is concerned with in the areas of defence, law and order, and foreign policy are much more specific to West Germany. They are sensitive areas, in which political action is taken only with a very acute awareness of the influence of the immediate past and the strategic and geographical situation of the Federal Republic.

Problems of law and order, unrest, protests and demonstrators, civil liberties and the Emergency Laws (*Notstandgesetze*) are intensified by the lingering memories of the Weimar and Nazi periods, and the anxieties which foreign observers express over the slightest deviation from democratic procedures and measures. The Federal Republic, because of Germany's past, is judged by a very rigorous standard in such matters. Democracy must not only exist, it must be seen to exist! So the banning of political parties, the rise of the NPD,[13] the Emergency Laws with their echoes of Article 48 of the Weimar constitution, the treatment of protesters, the protection of civil liberties in the courts – all these and similar problems are seized on in the foreign Press and the questions are put again: is Bonn really Weimar?; are the Nazis still in power?; are the Germans capable of becoming democrats? Such foreign attention tends to feed back into West Germany, and gives rise to parliamentary questions, Press and broadcasting comment, academic polemics,[14] and so on, to an extent which the problems themselves would not merit in any other

[13] See, for instance, a report of the Ministry of the Interior, mentioning the fact that the failure of the NPD to be represented in the 6th *Bundestag* had been noted with pleasure abroad (*Jahresbericht der Bundesregierung 1969*, p. 147).

[14] For example, K. Jaspers, *Wohin treibt die Bundesrepublik?* (Munich, 1966).

democracy. For, judged by the standards applied to other states, West Germany does not have a bad record in such matters. The Emergency Laws are a prominent example. In 1956 a constitutional amendment (Art. 59(*a*) of the Basic Law) was passed regarding the possibility of the declaration of war and the consequent division of powers among the various branches of the Government. Between 1956 and 1965 various other laws, not involving constitutional amendment, were promulgated, involving, for example, civil defence, traffic regulation and public utilities in emergencies. The major controversy was aroused over the proposals by the Grand Coalition for more comprehensive legislation, involving constitutional changes which the Government could undertake with its large majority. These proposals involved the definition of occasions of external and internal emergency, the preservation of parliamentary participation through the foundation of a 'miniature parliament' consisting of twenty-two members of the *Bundestag* and eleven members of the *Bundesrat,* and the statement of the powers of this committee, the President and the Government during the emergency. In particular, safeguards were devised for terminating emergency decrees within six months of the end of the emergency, and protecting the inviolability of the Basic Law and the Constitutional Court. It is true, as one commentator has pointed out,[15] that there remain unsatisfactory ambiguities of language, such as the phrases setting out types of internal emergency, including 'grave accident' and 'threat to the integrity of the democratic order', and that there is a case for the closer restriction of executive powers in internal emergencies, but the laws themselves bear favourable comparison with those of other democracies, in their careful protection of the rights of the elected assembly and their limitations on executive discretion. Yet trade unions, students, members of the FDP and SPD, the churches and various other organisations and sections of society tried to prevent these laws from being passed. Such vehement reaction is explicable, not so much by reference to the actual content of the Emergency Laws, as in terms of a sensitivity to the uses made in the past of such provisions, and a compulsion to present the best possible

[15] C. Schweitzer, 'Emergency Powers in the Federal Republic of Germany', *Western Political Quarterly,* XXII 1 (Mar. 1969) 112–21.

democratic image to the rest of the world. Whether such a 'holier than thou' attitude, even if demanded by foreign opinion, is dangerous in the longer term to West Germany's survival as a democracy is a question that is not answered by the protesters and critics.

The internal security of the Federal Republic becomes a matter of political controversy particularly in relation to two other problems: anti-Semitism and the sporadic reappearance of ex-Nazis, some with criminal charges outstanding against them, in public office. Anti-Semitism finds little overt expression today, and when it does, public opinion is easily roused against it, as in the outbreak of daubings of anti-Jewish slogans in 1959–60.[16] The Federal Republic's determined recognition of Israel as proper recipient of reparation payments was a matter of some controversy, but in general anti-Semitism appears to be one of the less obvious legacies of the Nazi past, though this verdict must be linked with the recognition that today there are very few Jews still remaining in the population. The hundreds of thousands of former Nazis who survived the war did not disappear, however. Many were subject to the de-Nazification procedures of the occupation forces,[17] but others escaped the net and often obtained high posts in the Government and civil service, the military, the judiciary and other areas of public life. Their unmasking, sometimes on the basis of evidence doled out strategically by the East German authorities, gives ammunition to those who see a revival of Nazism as inevitable, or who fear a well-hidden Nazi conspiracy to throw aside the democratic trappings of the present regime and restore a version of the Third *Reich*. Three points must be mentioned concerning this problem. First, the evidence suggests that the Russian occupation authorities made at least as much use of former Nazis in the Eastern zone as did the Allies in the Western zones, and the German Democratic Republic is in no position to cast stones westward on this count. Secondly, as the years pass fewer and fewer former Nazis who occupied responsible positions are still of an age to be active in public life in the Bonn Republic; a Nazi aged thirty in 1939 would be well over sixty

[16] W. Stahl (ed.), *The Politics of Postwar Germany* (New York, 1963) pp. 309–38: 'The Anti-Semitic Daubings in the Winter of 1959–60'.

[17] FitzGibbon, *Denazification*.

years old today. Thirdly, the Nazi Party was a complex and disparate collection of various types of individual, with different ideas and programmes, held together by Hitler's leadership and then by the exigencies of war. Today it is unlikely that Nazism as such could have survived or could revive. Danger there may be from right-wing extremists, but such dangers may have little or no connection with the political movements of the past, but rather may be phenomena of industrial societies in the present age.[18]

The importance of defence and military policies as political issues in the Federal Republic may be taken as a reliable indicator of the extent to which West Germany has made the transition from being a state 'on probation' in the world community, to one which is self-confident, able to make an effective contribution to the Western Alliance, and in which the past serves as a warning against which to compare the present.

Militarism was regarded by the Allies as one of the major causes of the two world wars in which Germany was the aggressor. The failure of Germany to observe the disarmament clauses of the Versailles Treaty made the Allies determined to ensure that, after the Second World War, disarmament would be a reality. Even in 1949, when the Federal Republic was formed, it was as a state without armed forces of its own, reliant on occupation forces for its external security. Three developments forced a reappraisal of this situation on the Western powers and on the Federal Republic itself. The cold war, particularly the increase in Russian military forces in Eastern Europe and the policies which Russia pursued in its satellite states, made for international tension. Secondly, the Russians created a para-military 'People's Police' in East Germany which was to all intents and purposes an Army. Thirdly, the Korean War which broke out in 1950 showed what could happen to a partitioned state if the Communist-dominated section should seek to absorb the non-Communist section. Besides, the calls of this war on the armed forces of the United States and Britain made more imperative a West

[18] E. Scheuch and H. Klingemann, 'Theorie des Rechtsradikalismus in westlichen Industriegesellschaften', in H. Ortlieb and B. Molitor (eds), *Hamburger Jahrbuch für Wirtschafts- und Gesellschaftspolitik, 1967* (Tübingen, 1967).

German contribution to the defence of Western Europe. As one of the chief architects of West Germany's new armed forces put it: 'we have become a border country of the free world'.[19] So, against the resistance of important sections of the community in Britain, France and in Germany itself (the SPD under Schumacher were strongly opposed), as well as against the automatic responses of 'the revival of fascist aggression' from east of the Iron Curtain, plans were made for the creation of new German armed forces.

At first, it was intended that West Germany's troops be integrated into a new European Defence Community – the 'Pleven Plan' – but after a long period of waiting, the French National Assembly in 1954 refused ratification of the agreements to implement this plan. So, in October 1954, the 'Paris Agreements' were signed by which the Federal Republic was admitted as a sovereign state into the North Atlantic Treaty Organisation, to make her own contribution of troops to that alliance.

In 1950 Chancellor Adenauer had appointed Theodor Blank as the official with the responsibility for dealing with questions of preparation for West German rearmament, should it be decided upon by the Allies. 'The preparatory phase of German rearmament was, first of all, marked by the fact that a new political and intellectual basis for the future German forces had to be found.'[20] For it was certain that neither the Allies nor West German public opinion would accept a West German Army that resembled, in its relation to the state and society or in its internal operation, the *Wehrmacht* of the Nazis or the *Reichswehr* of the pre-Hitler period. Baudisson identified the key problem thus: 'In my view, the idea of democratic armed forces consists simply of three things: organic integration of the army into the democratic state; devotion of its leaders to the state and its constitution; identity of values in the army and in the democratic state.'[21]

The relations of the military to society and the state have taken many forms in German history, but for most of the period until 1945 the military, though in many ways separa-

[19] Count Wolf Baudisson, 'The New German Army', *Foreign Affairs*, XXXIV 1 (Oct. 1955) 2.

[20] E. Waldman, *The Goose Step is Verboten: The German Army Today* (New York, 1964) p. 25.

[21] Baudisson, 'The New German Army', p. 3.

ted from the state, possessed great potential influence on political decisions. Not only was military action the basis on which Germany was unified, but under the Empire the military was regarded as the 'school of the nation', the repository of the virtues of patriotism, determination and obedience that were so highly regarded by the Kaiser and the Junkers. The Army increased in political importance in the 1914–18 war, and was called on to maintain the republican regime during the unrest of 1918–19, and in the face of later threats to the Weimar Republic's existence. Hitler gained control of the armed forces, but their role in the 'July plot' showed that this control was never complete. But the Bonn Republic was founded without an Army, and the reconstruction of military units required some very careful plans to be drawn up for 'integrating' the armed forces into society, and making their organisation and control congruent with the democratic order.[22] Formal legal control rests with the Defence Minister in peace-time, and the Chancellor in war-time. Both are politically responsible to the *Bundestag*. Parliamentary control of the armed forces is exercised through the constructive vote of no confidence in the Chancellor (which, if carried, compels the resignation of the Defence Minister along with the rest of the Government), through close and detailed budgetary control of military appropriations, and through the special defence committee of the *Bundestag*, which is a permanent committee with investigatory powers and can undertake inquiries on its own, as well as on the *Bundestag*'s, initiative. In addition, there is a Parliamentary Commissioner for the Armed Forces (*Wehrbeauftragter*), a kind of military Ombudsman,[23] with the task of investigating complaints from members of the armed forces or from other sources, concerning a variety of matters, such as allegations of the violation of the civil rights of soldiers.

Two associated concepts of the military–state relationship are *innere Führung* and, included within that notion, the idea of the 'citizen in uniform'. *Innere Führung* has been stated to consist of the acceptance of the idea of primacy of the

[22] Stahl (ed.), *The Politics of Postwar Germany*, pp. 249–70: 'Militarism in the Federal Republic?'.

[23] D. Rowat (ed.), *The Ombudsman* (London, 1965) chap. 5, 'West Germany's Military Ombudsman' by E. Lohse.

political over military control of the armed forces, the integration of the armed forces in a free and law-based state, the notion of the citizen in uniform, the legal protection of the individual's personality even in the special dependency-relationship that characterises the soldier, attention to the dignity of the individual, even under principles of command and obedience, and the acceptance of public law concerning the military as the basis of military order.[24] Other aspects of *inner Führung* are the political education of the soldier so that he can be aware of the broader context in which military action may have to occur, e.g. by an appreciation of the distinctions between the democratic and authoritarian forms of political regime, and the safeguarding of the rights of the soldier to participate in politics, within certain specific limits necessary to the preservation of discipline, etc., as voter, party supporter, candidate, or in any other way open to the citizen under the constitution. These are some aspects of the notion of the 'citizen in uniform'. Other aspects include the development of new and co-operative types of leadership to replace the old-model style which demanded unthinking obedience; the democratisation of military organisation; the linking of military and civilian occupations where these are of a technical nature, so that trades learned in the Army, for instance, can be applied in civilian life when Army service is over; and the transmission to the soldier of the notion of military service as a form of service to the community.[25]

Other aspects of the military which were and still are politically controversial include the problem of the selection of former officers by means of a special screening committee to check the personal and political characteristics of applicants; conscription and conscientious objection (safeguarded by the Basic Law, but being used to an increasing degree by draftees); the equipment and preparedness of the armed forces (for example, the problem of the Starfighters which seem to crash with alarming frequency!); the question of atomic weapons;[26] the offset costs for Allied troops stationed in West

[24] *Jahresbericht der Bundesregierung 1969*, p. 369.

[25] On *innere Führung* see Waldman, *The Goose Step is Verboten*, pt 2.

[26] President Heinemann has stated that the introduction of legislation for the purpose of giving the German armed forces their own atomic weapons would probably mean his refusal to sign the bill (*Die Welt*, 30 June 1969).

Germany;[27] and the observation of tendencies for members of the military to be associated with right-wing radical groups. The 1970 White Book on defence summed up the situation by admitting that the military had its deficiencies and problems, but that these were for a large part the deficiencies and problems of the society from which it was drawn. It cannot be easy to control satisfactorily an Army of nearly half a million troops, over half of which are conscripts, with an additional 100,000 reservists being called for exercises during the year. But despite its problems, the West German Army is now apparently well integrated in the democratic order of the Bonn Republic, and though the parties may differ over detail and over emphasis, defence policies are not really matters for intense partisan conflict in West Germany.

EXTERNAL RELATIONS

Foreign affairs have played a unique role in determining the policies and politics of West Germany since the Second World War. Because of West Germany's special position with regard to international relations, it is not surprising that it is in this area that party differences are at their most extreme, and the problems of the Federal Republic most clearly differentiated from those of other Western states. Germany itself was governed by representatives of foreign states until 1949, and even after 1949 certain foreign-imposed limitations on the sovereignty of the Federal Republic lingered on, with regard to defence and foreign policies, for example. The effects of the cold war, the absorption of East Germany into the Warsaw Pact alliance and the Russian-dominated East European economic system, and the formation of influential international organisations such as NATO and the EEC have provided the parameters within which Bonn's external relations have been conducted. These relations fall into three broad categories: those with West Germany's eastern neighbours, especially Russia, East Germany and Poland – the *Ostpolitik*; those with the Western allies of the Federal Republic, especially the United States, the United Kingdom and the members of the European Community; and those with the developing states of the 'third world'.

After the unwavering policies of Adenauer in favour of

[27] *Jahresbericht der Bundesregierung 1969*, p. 385.

alliance with the Western powers and firm hostility in the face of threats and blandishments from Russia's client-state, the DDR, a change to a more flexible eastern policy was distinguishable in 1961, when Adenauer and several of his colleagues appealed publicly for a Germany reunified under conditions of peace and freedom. This orientation towards a more positive reunification policy was continued under Erhard's Chancellorship. As this approach coincided generally with the position of the SPD at the time, and with the later appointment of the SPD leader, Brandt, as Foreign Minister, it was not surprising that the *Ostpolitik* of the Grand Coalition should have been one of the areas about which there seemed little controversy within the Government at the time. Rhetoric might have its own optimism, but realism demanded that any progress towards reunification, or even towards improved relations with the 'other Germany', be dependent upon a relaxation of tensions between East and West in the cold war, and a simultaneous effort at a more friendly relationship with the USSR – even, if possible, with Poland and other Warsaw Pact countries. Such progress seemed easiest to achieve within the area of trading relations. The visits of the Romanian Foreign Minister to West Germany and Brandt to Romania in 1967, for instance, produced a determination to emphasise 'meaningful progress in the areas of economic, technological and cultural collaboration, tourism and the strengthening of exchange visits and contacts between representatives of both countries'.[28] Other developments occurred on similarly pragmatic lines, attempting the possible and avoiding pressing for the unattainable. In January 1968 diplomatic relations were resumed with Yugoslavia, for example. The Russian invasion of Czechoslovakia in 1968 inevitably slowed such progress towards better relations, but by the time the 1969 elections were held the net effect was that a considerable movement towards an easing of tensions between West Germany and Eastern Europe had taken place, and there was a heightened awareness on the part of the West German voter that reunification was not to be attained by wishful thinking or nationalistic shibboleths.

[28] Communiqué following the visit of Brandt to Romania, 8 Aug. 1967, printed in B. Meissner (ed.), *Die deutsche Ostpolitik 1961–70: Kontinuität und Wandel* (Köln, 1970) pp. 218–19.

During the election campaign, the FDP and the SPD declared their readiness to undertake new initiatives in the relationships between the Federal Republic and the Warsaw Pact countries. The CDU speakers were generally more cautious on the question, emphasising the need, particularly after the 'Brezhnev Doctrine', to obtain some genuine indication from Moscow that the Soviet Union was ready to make concessions in return for a 'normalisation' of relations, and prepared to encourage a *rapprochement* between the two parts of Germany.

In the Government Declaration after the election, Brandt claimed for the Germans the same right of self-determination that was demanded by peoples in other countries. He spoke of the need for new forms of collaboration between the two parts of Germany, and its importance for peace in Europe and East–West relations. He suggested Government-level talks between the Federal Republic and the DDR, and pressed the Western powers to ameliorate the Berlin situation by talks with Russia. Other sections of the Declaration dealt with the improvement of relations with East European states, including, more specifically in the short term, a response to the proposal of the USSR for talks on a treaty of non-aggression, and the commencement of conversations with the Polish Government. Kiesinger, in his reply to the Declaration, stressed the willingness of the CDU to agree to the search for means of self-determination for the German people, but inveighed against any notion of recognising the existence of a 'second German state', and warned against a policy of 'illusion' with regard to the Soviet Union, particularly in the light of their action against Czechoslovakia. This debate set the tone of the two parties for the next eighteen months: the Government pursuing every chance of positive improvements in their relations with the East, even at the cost of neglect of the programme of domestic reform which they had promised, and the opposition parties continually reminding the Government of the untrustworthy nature of Soviet diplomacy and pointing to the lack of any substantive benefits to West Germany from talks with Russia, East Germany or Poland.

The Moscow Treaty, signed by Brandt, Scheel, Kosygin and Gromyko on 12 August 1970 after a long series of negotiations by members of the West German and Russian Governments, was a brief agreement on the part of the two states not to resort to force in their relations with each other, and by which they mutually recognised the territorial integrity of all European states in their existing boundaries, including specific mention of the Oder–Neisse line and the border between the two Germanys. A separate note from Scheel, the West German Foreign Minister, stated the Federal Republic's understanding that the treaty did not rule out the eventual possibility of a reunified Germany through free self-determination. Care was also taken to ensure that the three Western powers, the United States, France and Britain, appreciated that the treaty was not intended to limit their rights or responsibilities in relation to Germany as a whole, or to Berlin.

Meanwhile, earlier in 1970, talks were arranged between Brandt and Stoph, the Prime Minister of the DDR, the first of which took place in Erfurt in March. These talks were followed by a somewhat less happy session in Kassel in May, when the flag of the DDR was destroyed by demonstrators during the meeting. In both cases, the differences between the two sides could be summarised thus: the DDR wanted recognition by the Federal Republic of their legitimate existence as a state, prior to negotiations on the improvement of contacts and relations between the two Germanys; the Federal Republic was only willing to discuss recognition as part of a more general package of proposals for improved relations. A third round of talks was suggested, and after the Moscow Treaty Russia was clearly applying pressure for the East Germans to be more co-operative, but by mid-1971 further progress had been minimal. Meanwhile, four-power talks were held concerning Berlin, but the East Germans continued to obstruct periodically traffic between West Berlin and the Federal Republic.

The third specific target of the new Government's *Ostpolitik* was Poland, and a less dramatic but painstaking and patient series of talks took place between representatives of the two Governments, which resulted, in November 1970, in Chancellor Brandt visiting Warsaw to sign a treaty with Poland which recognised the reality of the Oder–Neisse border established at the end of the war. While in Warsaw, Brandt suddenly went on his knees in front of a memorial to the Jews of the Warsaw Ghetto – a gesture which aroused great controversy in West Germany and which added to the sharp debate on the propriety and wisdom of 'signing away part of German territory', the area under Polish administration pending the signing of a peace treaty with Germany.

Only time can judge the wisdom of the more flexible, often risk-laden policies towards Eastern Europe which the Brandt coalition has undertaken, just as time will reveal their effects. Brandt promised that his policies would consist of both continuity and renovation. Certainly there are elements of both present in the *Ostpolitik* of the Brandt Government. However, in terms of short-term improvement in the relationships with Eastern Europe, it is to be doubted whether these conversations and treaties will achieve as much as increased trading and cultural links are doing already, and yet the price in terms of domestic politics has been high. Not only have the attentions of leading members of the Government been taken up disproportionately with the negotiations at the cost of neglect of internal reform but in addition party controversy has been sharpened, the coalition put at risk through FDP defections and endangered by the possibility of denial of ratification of the Moscow and Warsaw Treaties by the *Bundestag*. Yet the image of the SPD–FDP coalition as an active and imaginative Government has been improved, and West German politics might be the beneficiary from the sharpened party debate which has resulted, and the removal of illusions about the impermanence of the Oder–Neisse line.

The Brandt Government emphasised in its Government Declaration the continued attachment of the Federal Republic to the Western Alliance and its support for a wider European Community. Such explicit avowals were politically wise, to protect the first socialist-dominated post-war administration from charges that it was pursuing a course of neutralism, or even 'socialist solidarity', in its approaches to the USSR and the DDR.

Not that these Western aspects of external policy are themselves trouble-free. The North Atlantic Treaty Organisation, though as old as the Federal Republic, unlike the Bonn Republic has been weakened rather than strengthened by the passage of time. Europe has ceased, for the time being at least, to be the major crisis region in the East–West conflict; Southeast Asia and the Middle East have replaced it. France, during de Gaulle's period in power, loosened its ties to NATO. Britain and the United States have had squabbles with the Federal Republic over offset payments to balance some of the foreign exchange costs involved in retaining their troops in the Federal Republic, particularly as their foreign exchange problems have contrasted with the strength of the *Deutschmark* recently. America's preoccupation with Vietnam has had repercussions on her interest and involvement in NATO. The treaty assented to by the major powers restricting the spread of nuclear weapons has caused controversy in West Germany over whether, if West Germany ratifies the treaty, her research and development of atomic energy for peaceful purposes would be hampered. The changing scope of the NATO alliance, the growing strength of West Germany's own armed forces and the general reduction in tension in Central Europe have, over the past two decades, altered quite fundamentally the relationship between the Federal Republic and her allies, and it will be a task of the present Government to respond to these changes by developing new, and perhaps more independent, policies towards Western Europe and the United States, even at the cost of conflict with the CDU. But though the parties differ on details of the form such relations should take in the future, and though there exists an anti-Americanism of the right as well as of the left in West German politics, there is a consensus that America still constitutes the Federal Republic's major protection against aggression, and that relationships with the United States are at the heart of West German foreign policy.

The success story of the Common Market in the 1960s, and its subsequent stagnation and difficulties, have been increasingly influential in the shaping of West Germany's external policies. Economically, West Germany has benefited considerably from the existence of the European Economic Community. Politically, the Community has grown into a regional bloc of great potential – with provision in the Rome Treaty for progress towards political unity. The attempts by Britain to secure entry have generally secured unstinting support from West German Governments, for Britain would add to the resources of the Community and would act as a counterweight to French dominance. But, on the debit side, the Community has caused difficulties for West German agriculture (especially dairy produce, and, more recently, through the new marketing agreements for wine); should reunification ever become a realistic possibility West German membership of the EEC might be a major obstacle (as it is, the East European emphasis of Brandt's foreign and commercial policies has stimulated objections from other members of the Community); and the requirement that the economic, social, transport, labour and other policies of the Community members eventually be harmonised, if not integrated, is used as an excuse for preventing change by parties and pressure-groups opposed to certain policies, and imposes a degree of additional uncertainty concerning the future which constrains policy planning.

West Germany's foreign policy has also become increasingly concerned with the problems of the 'third world' and with opportunities for the contribution of development aid. Though, at first, there were indications that such aid was closely interlinked with the Federal Republic's interest in limiting the advance of Communism in the underdeveloped regions of the world, later statements have stressed that, as a basic political principle, development aid should not be used as a means of political pressure. To co-ordinate development policies and implement aid programmes, a Ministry of Economic Co-operation was created in 1961. The Government also makes use of non-state organisations and private agencies for distributing aid: the churches, private foundations, and foundations which are 'daughter organisations' of the political parties – the Konrad Adenauer, Friedrich Ebert and Friedrich Naumann Foundations.[29] Voluntary service in developing countries by young people is encouraged by legal recognition of it as equivalent to military service. Apart from the special case of Israel, which has received special payments under the reparations (*Wiedergutmachung*) pact of 1952, Latin America, North Africa and Asia have been areas of greatest concentration of West German assistance. Not only has West Germany's development policy humanitarian and strategic aims; it is also of advantage to West German trade

[29] On the controversial nature of the recipients of aid from these Foundations, including 'freedom fighters' and guerrillas, see H. Vahlefeld, 'Entwicklungshilfe als Bumerang?', *Die Welt*, 28 Nov. 1970.

relations with underdeveloped states, and it can serve as a legitimate means of waking the 'creative strength' of Germany's younger generation and linking it to large-scale projects for the future.[30]

[30] The point is taken from W. Besson, *Die Aussenpolitik der Bundesrepublik* (Munich, 1970) p. 454.

12 Society and Politics in West Germany

POLITICS AND THE SOCIAL SYSTEM

It has been stressed throughout this book that the politics of West Germany must be understood as a compound of particular historical forces – the 'German' aspects – and the influences that are common to all modern, industrialised societies. These factors are relevant to the political structures, processes and policies of the Federal Republic; they are also influences on the social, economic and cultural systems, and in this way have an indirect effect on the political system. Religious divisions, regional loyalties, the types and distribution of industry and agriculture, the social structure, the educational system – all are explicable by reference to Germany's past and to the imperatives of industrial society. All are, at times and in a variety of ways, relevant to the explanation of West Germany's politics. It must be remembered therefore, in discussing the politics of the Federal Republic, that no aspect of politics is isolated from the influences of the past, nor from the effects of the contemporary environment, whether in terms of the policies of other states, the spread of international business enterprises, the 'internationalisation' of student protest, the development of the Common Market, international currency problems or whatever. Bearing this in mind, two final questions must be raised. In what directions is the West German political system developing? And is this system in fact democratic?

THE POLITICAL DEVELOPMENT OF WEST GERMANY

Political development is not just an attribute of the countries of the 'third world'. It is a quality of any political system which is successfully adapting to the stresses to which it is subjected, and evolving new capacities for coping with problems. The Federal Republic is thus, in a number of ways, a 'developing country' in political and social terms. Though only just over twenty years have passed since its foundation, the current regime seems to be the most stable since the end of the Second Empire, and to have developed a high degree of capability of adaptation to the social and political changes that have occurred in recent years, inside and outside the Federal Republic. Economic crises have occurred, diplomatic pressures have been applied, the right-wing radical parties and the left-wing 'extra-parliamentary opposition' have challenged the political authorities, social stresses have resulted from increasing urban growth and industrial development, refugees and foreign workers have been assimilated. Any of these problems might have seriously weakened the viability of the regime, but it has survived them all, aided by various forms of external support, it is true, but also because the post-war political culture is itself different from that of the Weimar period, and is more compatible with the arrangements of the political system. Politically, as well as economically, West Germany has 'caught up' with its Western neighbours.

Predictions about the political future are always hazardous, particularly as they concern Germany. The short life of the 'Thousand-Year *Reich*' and the swift recovery of West Germany from defeat in 1945 illustrate this. But if the assessment of West Germany as a 'developed' political system is correct, then certain trends may be distinguished which concern the future.

First, it would appear that the 'provisional' regime that exists in West Germany at the moment might, despite the intentions of its founders,[1] prove more durable than any of its predecessors. There seems to be little overt internal hostility to the democratic order; quasi-autonomous social groups which have weakened the authority of the state in the past – industry, the military and the bureaucracy, for example – are now more closely integrated into the state; the regime itself has not been associated directly with military or economic disaster, as were its predecessors; the multiplicity of international ties which West Germany now has will tend to be supportive of the *status quo*; and finally, the hopes cherished by the authors of the Basic Law of eventual reunification have

[1] The preamble to the Basic Law speaks of it as giving a 'new order to political life for a transitional period'.

lessened with the years, so the likelihood of the assimilation of the Federal Republic into a reunified German state is small.

Changes in the political system have taken place. The dominance of the Chancellor and his Cabinet within the system, the trend towards a two-party *Bundestag* based on stricter party discipline, have made the West German legislature an institution more for the persuasion of the public of the merits of the case than the place where decisions are actually taken. The *Bundestag* thus fulfils an information function rather than a decision-making function.[2] The parties themselves have broadened their membership and support by taking less narrow or ideologically oriented positions on issues – again a trend in keeping with the 'end of ideology' in other democratic states. Proposals for reorganising the federal structure, changing the electoral system, even rewriting the Basic Law entirely have been made.[3] But such changes would be adaptive. They would not, in themselves, have the effect of changing the federal, republican and democratic system of government in West Germany.

Secondly, there does seem to be a clear tendency towards increasing political intervention and control in more and more areas of society. Simultaneously, new planning and administrative techniques are being developed, partly in the cause of greater efficiency, partly in order to introduce a greater degree of predictability and control in areas where the costs of uncertainty are high: public spending, educational planning, the planning of transport facilities, scientific research and development, housing, manpower policy and similar concerns. Horst Ehmke has suggested one reason for this development:

> This extremely complex system of modern industrial society has become altogether dependent on the decisions and achievements of the political system. But precisely on account of this dependency democratic politics must appear, to the specialised organisations in society and the economy, to be a potentially incalculable disturbance fac-

[2] H. Schmidt, 'Die Macht der Information', *Die Zeit*, 25 Dec. 1970.

[3] The suggestion to make a total revision of the Basic Law in order to take account of the social changes of the past two decades has been made, for instance, by H. Dichgans, a CDU member of the *Bundestag*, in his article 'Ist unsere Verfassung tabu?', *Die Zeit*, 27 Feb. 1970.

tor, which, in the interests of co-ordination and planning, must be brought as far as possible under control.[4]

The multiplication of advisory committees, planning units, experts in governmental employment, the growing utilisation of electronic data-processing equipment, techniques of calculation and forecasting, the development of academic disciplines such as 'futurology' and policy analysis, all are associated with this trend.[5]

The long-term political effects of this development, which is by no means confined to the West German political system, seem most likely to be of two types. There is a danger of democracy being replaced by 'technocracy' – rule by experts.[6] At present, this danger is minimised by the defenders of increased political planning, on the grounds that they desire only the improvement of the information base for political decision-making, and the better co-ordination of political resources. Nevertheless, suspicion lingers, and doubts about data-banks, the usurpation of political responsibility by experts and administrators, and the manipulation of the public, are increasing. But there is also the possibility that one consequence of increased political planning will be the removal of secondary and detailed questions from the arena of political debate as they become matters for expert diagnosis, leaving more time and energy for the discussion of more basic questions of political principle: the proper extent of state intervention in the economy; the balance between individual freedom and social responsibility; the rights and obligations of property ownership; the goals of foreign policy; and so on. This, in turn, may sharpen again the distinctions between the major parties and revive political interest among the general public by simplifying what is, at present, often a very complex level of public political discourse.

[4] H. Ehmke, 'Die Generation, auf die wir gewartet haben', in *Politik der praktischen Vernunft* (Frankfurt, 1969) p. 201.

[5] On the development of these in Germany, see K. Lompe, 'Die Neugestaltung von Regierung und Verwaltung in der Bundesrepublik Deutschland', *Mitteilungen des Instituts für Gesellschaftspolitik in Wien,* I (Mar. 1970) 13–35; and K. Lompe, 'The Role of Scientific Planning in the Government Process: The West German Experience', *American Journal of Economics and Sociology*, XXIX 4 (Oct. 1970) 369–87.

[6] Attention is drawn to this problem of 'systemism' by R. Dahrendorf, 'Sozialismus oder Liberalismus', in C. Grossner *et al.* (eds.), *Das 198 Jahrzent, Eine Team-Prognose für 1970 bis 1980* (Hamburg, 1969) pp. 346–7.

Thirdly, West Germany is becoming 'excessively normal',[7] especially in terms of its political culture. The similarities between West Germany and France, Britain and America are increasing, and exceed those between the two sections of the old Germany. The special and distinctive aspects of the political culture of pre-war Germany have, after a quarter of a century, lost their importance. 'Wars always produce other results than those for which they were fought.'[8] The war for the assertion of German culture has resulted in its dilution in the cultures of the Atlantic West and the Slavonic East. The refugees have been assimilated, and are declining in political significance. Regional loyalties are less of a political factor than at any time in the past. Apart from foreign policy, the major political issues and the norms of the political culture which are transferred by political socialisation are more and more similar to those of other Western democracies. The European Community is acquiring increasing political significance for West Germany, as it is for its other member-states. The West German citizen is becoming more and more a 'political animal', interested in politics, and even if this interest is not expressed in the membership figures of political parties, it is indicated by the readership of political books and journals, by audience figures for television programmes of a political nature, by an increased willingness to discuss politics in private and in public. And these changes are themselves perhaps a sign of the growing stability of democratic politics in West Germany.

WEST GERMANY: A DEMOCRACY?

> The Federal Republic of Germany is a democratic and social federal state.
>
> All state authority emanates from the people . . .[9]

For the extreme left, West Germany is not and never has been a democracy, because it is a society still controlled by a privileged minority, whether called an elite, a ruling class, or a

[7] The phrase is from A. Grosser, *Deutschlandbilanz, Geschichte Deutschlands seit 1945* (Munich, 1970) p. 499.

[8] R. Hochhuth, *The Representative*, trans. by R. D. MacDonald (Penguin ed., Harmondsworth, 1969) pp. 124–5.

[9] The Basic Law, Art. 20, ss. 1 and 2.

politico-military-industrial complex.[10] The Federal Republic is a capitalist society, and capitalism, for the extreme left, is by definition incompatible with democracy. For the extreme right, whether of an ultra-conservative or a radical type, West Germany *is* a democracy, and that, in their view, is just what is wrong. A democracy is divisive, open to conflict, lacks leadership, pride and national self-consciousness. More moderate opinion would have to judge the political system of West Germany by other standards, and a reasonable verdict in those terms would seem to be that, though there are still non-democratic elements of political life which can be identified, and while many of these aspects require very close scrutiny even today, on the whole the structures and processes of West German politics are democratic, and, indeed, in many ways more so than in any other European state.

The Basic Law provides a framework of norms and rules, many of which are specifically designed to protect and nurture democracy: the guarantees of freedom of speech, opinion, assembly and religion; safeguards for the autonomy of the *Länder*; the powers of the Constitutional Court, etc. The electoral and party laws are democratic in form and in operation, though both are capable of amendment without necessarily affecting their democratic orientation. West German political parties seem to be at least as democratic internally as those in other countries.[11] The citizen has guaranteed channels of redress against administrative impropriety. The military is hedged about with protective limitations on its internal operation in the name of democracy, even at the expense of its functional efficiency. Imperfections remain. For many reasons it would seem that the 'party oligarchies'[12] and the lobbies are over-influential in the political system. The Emergency Laws are capable of improvement, despite their careful attempts not to diminish parliamentary government. The constitutional possibility of banning political parties is not an unmixed blessing, and there is a danger of labelling critics of the current system as 'anti-democratic' when in fact

10 A discussion of this case is contained in U. Jaeggi, *Macht und Herrschaft in der Bundesrepublik* (Frankfurt, 1969).

11 See, for example, A. Gunlicks, 'Intraparty Democracy in West Germany: A Look at the Local Level', *Comparative Politics*, II 2 (Jan. 1970) 229–49.

12 The term is used by Jaspers, *Wohin treibt die Bundesrepublik?* pp. 139–40.

they are only recommending improvements of a more democratic nature.[13] Wire-tapping, the monopolistic structure of the opinion media, the powers of the police, are other areas of concern in discussions about West German democracy.

But these questions of structure, process and organisation will be secondary to the more fundamental problem of the commitment of the public to democracy as a means of making public decisions. Reforms of the Basic Law, the electoral system, the works councils, or the financing of political parties may all be influential, but ultimately it all depends on the citizen:

> So let us further develop the Basic Law, in so far as that seems, after careful examination, to be required. Let us not, however, forget that the political responsibility for our freedom and order lies not with the Basic Law, but with ourselves.[14]

[13] K. Sontheimer, 'Anti-Democratic Tendencies in Contemporary German Thought', *Political Quarterly*, XL 3 (July 1969) 268–82.

[14] Ehmke, 'Grundgesetz und politisches Handeln', in *Politik der praktischen Vernunft*, p. 156.

Appendices

A. Standing Committees of the *Bundestag*, 1969

B. The West German Cabinet, July 1971

C. Federal Election Results

D. *Land* Election Results, 1970–1

E. Chronological Guide

APPENDIX A

Standing Committees of the *Bundestag*, 1969

Committee	*Party of Chairman*
Interior	SPD
Procedure	SPD
Education	SPD
Youth	SPD
Economic co-operation	SPD
Agriculture	SPD
Labour	SPD
Transport	SPD
Economics	FDP
Budget	CDU–CSU
Finance	CDU–CSU
Defence	CDU–CSU
Foreign affairs	CDU–CSU
German affairs	CDU–CSU
Law	CDU–CSU
Petitions	CDU–CSU
Housing	CDU–CSU

APPENDIX B

The West German Cabinet, July 1971

Chancellor	Willy Brandt (SPD)
Foreign Minister	Walter Scheel (FDP)
Minister in the Chancellor's Department	Horst Ehmke (SPD)
Interior Minister	Hans-Dietrich Genscher (FDP)
Justice Minister	Gerhard Jahn (SPD)
Defence Minister	Helmut Schmidt (SPD)
Economics and Finance Minister	Karl Schiller (SPD)[1]
Agriculture Minister	Josef Ertl (FDP)
Labour Minister	Walter Arendt (SPD)
Transport Minister	Georg Leber (SPD)
Housing Minister	Lauritz Lauritzen (SPD)
Education Minister	Hans Leussink (non-party)
Minister for German Affairs	Egon Franke (SPD)
Minister for Economic Co-operation	Erhard Eppler (SPD)
Minister for Health, Family and Youth Affairs	Käte Strobel (SPD)

[1] The Ministries of Economics and Finance were merged in May 1971, following the resignation of the Finance Minister, Alex Möller.

APPENDIX C

Federal Election Results

	1949	*1953*	*1957*	*1961*	*1965*	*1969*
CDU–CSU	31·0	45·2	50·2	45·3	47·6	46·1
SPD	29·2	28·8	31·8	36·2	39·3	42·7
FDP	11·9	9·5	7·7	12·8	9·5	5·8
Other parties	27·9	16·5	10·3	5·7	3·6	5·4

APPENDIX D

Land Election Results, 1970–1

Land	*Date*	*Turnout* %	*CDU* %	*SPD* %	*FDP* %	*NPD* %	*Others* %
Hamburg	22 Mar. 70	73·5	32·8	55·3	7·1	2·7	2·1
North Rhine-Westphalia	14 June 70	73·6	46·3	46·1	5·5	1·1	1·0
Lower Saxony	14 June 70	76·7	45·7	46·2	4·4	3·2	0·4
Saarland	14 June 70	83·4	47·9	40·8	4·4	3·4	3·6
Hesse	8 Nov. 70	82·7	39·7	45·9	10·1	3·0	1·3
Bavaria	22 Nov. 70	80·1	56·4	33·3	5·5	2·9	1·9
West Berlin	14 Mar. 71	88·9	38·2	50·4	8·5	–	2·9
Rhineland-Pfalz	21 Mar. 71	79·3	50·0	40·5	5·9	2·7	0·9
Schleswig-Holstein	25 Apr. 71	79·2	51·7	41·2	3·8	1·3	2·0
Bremen	10 Oct. 71	80·0	31·6	55·3	7·1	2·8	3·1

APPENDIX E

Chronological Guide

1815	Germanic confederation created by Congress of Vienna.
1834	Establishment of *Zollverein* (customs union).
1848	National Assembly met at Frankfurt.
1862	Bismarck appointed Chief Minister of Prussia.
1864	Prussian war with Denmark.
1866	Austro-Prussian war.
1867	North German Federation founded.
1870–1	Franco-Prussian war.
1871	Proclamation of Second *Reich*.
1890	Bismarck resigns as Imperial Chancellor.
1914	Outbreak of First World War.
1918	Germany signs armistice ending the war. Kaiser William II abdicates. Germany proclaimed a republic.
1918–19	Spartacist revolt.
1919	National Assembly meets in Weimar to draft a constitution for the Republic. Ebert elected first President of the Weimar Republic.
1920	The Kapp *putsch*.
1922	Rapallo Treaty between Germany and Russia.
1923	Occupation of the Ruhr. Failure of Hitler's Munich *putsch*. Height of hyper-inflation of the currency.
1925	Hindenburg elected President. Locarno Treaty between Germany, Britain, France, Italy and Belgium.
1926	Germany enters League of Nations.
1929	Young Plan for dealing with reparations payments by Germany.
1930	Nazis secure 107 seats at general election.
1930–2	Minority Governments ruling by use of emergency powers.
1932	Hindenburg re-elected President. Nazis secure 230 seats in general election.
1933	Hitler appointed Chancellor. *Reichstag* fire. Nazis pass Enabling Act. Germany withdraws from League of Nations.
1934	'Night of the long knives' purge of SA and other elements of the Nazi Party.

1935 Nürnberg Laws against the Jews introduced.
1936 Occupation of the Rhineland by German troops. Axis Pact signed between Germany and Italy.
1938 *Anschluss* with Austria. Munich Agreement on German claims to parts of Czechoslovakia.
1939 German non-aggression pact with Russia. Invasion of Poland by German troops.
1939–45 Second World War.
1944 Allied invasion of Europe. 'July plot' against Hitler's life.
1945 Hitler commits suicide. Unconditional surrender of German armed forces. Allied occupation in four zones of Germany introduced. Potsdam Conference on the future of Germany.
1946 'Stuttgart speech' by American Secretary of State Byrnes indicating hopes of revival of German self-government.
1948 Currency reforms in Western zones. Berlin blockade by Russians and the 'airlift'. Elections to the Parliamentary Council in West Germany.
1949 Promulgation of the Basic Law. First elections to *Bundestag*. Adenauer elected Chancellor.
1953 Second elections to *Bundestag*.
1955 Restoration of full sovereignty to West German state. Federal Republic becomes member of NATO.
1956 Ban by Constitutional Court on Communist Party.
1957 Saar enters Federal Republic. Third *Bundestag* elections.
1961 Berlin Wall erected. Fourth elections to *Bundestag*.
1963 Erhard becomes Chancellor in place of Adenauer.
1965 Fifth *Bundestag* elections.
1966 Economic crisis. Kiesinger becomes Chancellor in place of Erhard. Grand Coalition formed.
1969 Sixth *Bundestag* elections. Brandt elected as Chancellor. Coalition formed between SPD and FDP.
1970 Meetings at Erfurt and Kassel between Brandt and Stoph, the Prime Minister of the DDR. Moscow Treaty signed between Germany and Russia. Warsaw Treaty signed between Germany and Poland.

Bibliography

INTRODUCTION

P. H. Merkl, *Germany, Yesterday and Tomorrow* (Oxford U.P., 1965).

HISTORICAL BACKGROUND: (i) pre-1945

W. S. Allen, *The Nazi Seizure of Power* (Eyre & Spottiswoode, 1966).

Ernest K. Bramstead, *Goebbels and National Socialist Propaganda* (Cresset Press, 1965).

A. Bullock, *Hitler: A Study in Tyranny* (Penguin Books, 1963).

Erich Eyck, *A History of the Weimar Republic* (Harvard U.P./Oxford U.P., vol I, 1962; vol. II, 1964).

Carl J. Friedrich, 'The Failure of a One-Party System: Hitler Germany', in Samuel P. Huntington and Clement H. Moore (eds), *Authoritarian Politics in Modern Society* (Basic Books, New York, 1970).

George L. Mosse, *The Crisis of German Ideology* (Weidenfeld & Nicolson, 1966).

Robert J. O'Neill, *The German Army and the Nazi Party, 1933–39* (Cassell, 1966).

E. Peterson, *The Limits of Hitler's Power* (Princeton U.P., 1969).

K. S. Pinson, *Modern Germany* (Collier-Macmillan, 2nd ed., 1966).

Terence Prittie, *Germans Against Hitler* (Hutchinson, 1964).

A. J. Ryder, *The German Revolution of 1918* (Cambridge U.P., 1967).

D. Schoenbaum, *Hitler's Social Revolution* (Weidenfeld & Nicolson, 1967).

Karl de Schweinitz, Jr, *Industrialisation and Democracy* (Free Press, New York, 1964) chap. 7: 'German Industrialisation: The Weakening of the Democratic Impulse'.

William L. Shirer, *The Rise and Fall of the Third Reich*

(Secker & Warburg, 1962).
A. J. P. Taylor, *Bismarck* (Hamish Hamilton, 1955).
R. M. Watt, *The Kings Depart* (Weidenfeld & Nicolson, 1969).

HISTORICAL BACKGROUND: (ii) post-1945

Konrad Adenauer, *Memoirs, 1945–53* (Weidenfeld & Nicolson, 1966).
Lucius D. Clay, *Decision in Germany* (Doubleday, New York; Heinemann, London, 1950).
Raymond Ebsworth, *Restoring Democracy in Germany: The British Contribution* (Stevens, 1960).
Lewis J. Edinger, *Kurt Schumacher* (Oxford U.P., 1965).
C. FitzGibbon, *Denazification* (Michael Joseph, 1969).
John Gimbel, *A German Community under American Occupation* (Stanford U.P., 1961).
W. F. Hanreider, *West German Foreign Policy, 1949–63* (Stanford U.P., 1967).
R. Hiscocks, *Democracy in West Germany* (Oxford U.P., 1963).
—— *Germany Revived: An Appraisal of the Adenauer Era* (Gollancz, 1966).
P. H. Merkl, *The Origin of the West German Republic* (Oxford U.P., 1963).
Walter Stahl (ed.), *The Politics of Postwar Germany* (Praeger, New York, 1963).
H. Wallich, *Mainsprings of the German Revival* (Yale U.P., 1955).

THE POLITICAL SYSTEM

Gerard Braunthal, *The Federation of German Industry in Politics* (Cornell U.P., 1965).
R. Bunn, *German Politics and the Spiegel Affair* (Louisiana State U.P., 1968).
Douglas A. Chalmers, *The Social Democratic Party of Germany* (Yale U.P., 1964).
Fritz Erler, *Democracy in Germany* (Harvard U.P., 1965).
Helga Grebing, *The History of the German Labour Movement* (Oswald Wolff, 1969).
Arnold J. Heidenheimer, *Adenauer and the CDU* (Nijhoff, The Hague, 1960).

Herbert Jacob, *German Administration since Bismarck* (Yale U.P., 1963).

O. Kirchheimer, 'Germany: The Vanishing Opposition', in R. Dahl (ed.), *Political Oppositions in Western Democracies* (Yale U.P., 1966).

U. W. Kitzinger, *German Electoral Politics* (Oxford U.P., 1960).

Gerhard Loewenberg, *Parliament in the German Political System* (Cornell U.P., 1967).

Edward L. Pinney, *Federalism, Bureaucracy and Party Politics in Western Germany: The Role of the Bundesrat* (Univ. of North Carolina Press, 1963).

R. J. C. Preece, *Land Elections in the German Federal Republic* (Longman, 1968).

POLITICAL CULTURE

G. Almond and S. Verba, *The Civic Culture* (Little, Brown, Boston, 1965).

G. D. H. Cole, *A History of Socialist Thought,* vol. IV (Macmillan, 1958) pt ii, chap. xx; vol. v (Macmillan, 1961) chap. ii.

R. Dahrendorf, *Society and Democracy in Germany* (Weidenfeld & Nicolson, 1968).

Hans Kohn, *The Mind of Germany* (Macmillan, 1965).

E. Nolte, *Three Faces of Fascism* (Weidenfeld & Nicolson, 1965).

S. Verba, 'Germany: The Remaking of a Political Culture', in L. Pye and S. Verba, *Political Culture and Political Development* (Princeton U.P., 1965).

MISCELLANEOUS

R. W. Leonhardt, *This Germany, the Story since the Third Reich* (Penguin Books, 1966).

William Manchester, *The Arms of Krupp* (Michael Joseph, 1969).

Index